Anonymous

The South Florida Railroad Co.

Gate City Route

Anonymous

The South Florida Railroad Co.
Gate City Route

ISBN/EAN: 9783337384388

Printed in Europe, USA, Canada, Australia, Japan

Cover: Foto ©Andreas Hilbeck / pixelio.de

More available books at **www.hansebooks.com**

THE
SOUTH FLORIDA RAILROAD CO.

Sanford to Tampa, Main Line,	. . . .	115 miles.
Pemberton Ferry Branch, Pemberton Ferry to Bartow,	·	57 "
Bartow Branch, Bartow Junction to Bartow,	. . .	17 "
Sanford and Indian River Railroad, Sanford to Lake Charm,	18 "
Total mileage,	. . . . .	207 miles.

OFFICERS:

JAS. E. INGRAHAM, President, Sanford, Fla.

R. M. PULSIFER, Vice-President, Boston, Mass.

B. R. SWOOPE, Supt. and Purchasing Agt., Sanford, Fla.

C. C. HASKELL, Treasurer, Sanford, Fla.

WILBUR McCOY, Auditor and Gen. Frt. and Ticket Agt., Sanford, Fla.

S. M. SPARKMAN, General Counsel for Co., Tampa, Fla.

J. D. STOCKTON, Traveling Agent, Tampa, Fla.

H. C. WHITEMAN, Traveling Agent, Sanford, Fla.

W. E. ARNOLD, Passenger Agent, Orlando, Fla.

PREPARED BY THE
PASSENGER DEPARTMENT
— OF —
THE SOUTH FLORIDA RAILROAD COMPANY.

ILLUSTRATED AND PRINTED BY THE SOUTH PUBLISHING COMPANY, 70 PARK PLACE, N. Y.

LAKE ONORO, ONORO STATION, D. P. R. R.

THE GARDENS OF THE HESPERIDES.

When the first frost paints, with singular fidelity, a Florida hamack on the window pane, the invalid and tourist searches his maps to learn some more about Florida. The stale legends of Ponce de Leon, and the much abused Melendez and his rival pall upon a fastidious appetite. "*Toujours perdrix*," growled the French bon vivant over his hundred and forty-fourth partridge. Let us see if we cannot do a little generalizing about Florida that will help the traveler to an independent opinion of its character and climate.

From a central point in its interior, about the latitude of Cape Canaveral, a hundred and eighty degrees east or west puts the point of the compass a little south of Lucknow, on the sub-peninsula formed by the Ganges and Brahmapootra. The two countries are very much alike. As the earth heels upon itself on our Gulf, swinging the wide loop of the equatorial current north and east, the great Asiatic current turns from its counter point, about the Indian coast, into the Japan current. The co-tidal wave, from its remote origin in the southwest Pacific strikes, like a great clock, at the same hour on the coasts of Hindostan and Florida. There is a corresponding physical likeness in the delta formed by these massive streams, to our Florida Everglades, that is repeated in the Run of Cutch at the mouth of the Indus. That these great alluvial plains should be characterized by a similarity in soil, climate and vegetation is the result of prime physical laws. Ninety degrees either way puts the point of the compass on the meridians of the Pacific Isles and the Mediterranean basin.

THE SOIL.

We may draw a more exact conclusion of the nature of the soil, in these favored latitudes, from the U. S. Consular reports on orange culture; for the vegetable production is the land's own expression of its nature. "The Orange does best," says the report from Porto Rico, "in a sandy soil." The soil of Valencia in Spain is described as "tribasic, cretaceous, with a strong admixture of sand, clay, loam." In Andalusia is "40 per cent. of sand." In Sidon, Asia, "light red, dark loam, sandy and clayey soils." In Morocco, "the orange grows luxuriantly in the sand." The soil of Florida is like that, cretaceous, tribasic, sandy, sometimes a loam and passing into a marl on the west coast or on low, shoaly rivers; but oftenest a sandy loam adapted to orange culture.

GEOLOGY AND TOPOGRAPHY.

The base of the system is the underlying secondary or orbitoidal limestone, bearing fossil of the same species found on the Run of Cutch, at the mouth of the Indus. The formation is sand or marl, over the rotten limestone, superimposed by the characteristic orbitoidal limestone. The over-

3

lying loam or marl is strongly impregnated with iron and sulphurets. There is a strong likeness in this chalk, to the soil about Rome, even to thermal springs, depositing travertin, found on Tampa bay, and sunken lakes and pools, like classic Fucinus, Julius Cæsar was planning to drain when Tu Brutis made a point against him. Shells, Meandrina, Pyrula, Cyrena, Venus Mercatoria, are found in the chalk rim of the great basin of Okeechobee and the Everglades; and the fossil of the tertiary in the valley of Peace Creek, include mammoth, mastodon, with bones of the manatee and huge birds.

The watershed, over hidden veins, permeating the dark underground aqueducts and corridors, with massive currents bursting out in full head at Wakulla, at Hoosier and Clay Springs in Orange, or disgorging at sea, suggests a curious resemblance, as if the surface reflected the scenes below. The dynamics of the system is very simple. The long peninsula, hung like an ear of Indian corn to the continent, is subdivided in low, shallow terraces. On and over these the water drops and pools, permeating the light, spongy soil, and falling again to a second low plateau, or catch basin, to be again stored and dispersed. It has resulted in bodies of water so numerous, so clarified by the light, porous soil, as to seem incredible for beauty and number. Each chosen area affects to be peculiarly blessed; yet, when we find 800 pools, from a surface of forty acres to several hundred square miles in Orange county alone, the peculiarity is less striking. But this characteristic is mainly limited to areas north of latitude 29 degrees north. The general form of the State is of a carpenter's square, fifty or sixty miles wide by 36 miles from Rio Perdido to Fernandina, and of a like depth to the Keys.

CLIMATE OF FLORIDA.

The same physical concurrents observed in treating of the soil of Florida have a comparative influence on the climate. The arrangement of the table of temperatures is by latitude and longitude of given centers in the great terrestrial Orange Belt.

COMPARATIVE TEMPERATURES IN THE ORANGE BELT.

COUNTRIES.	LATITUDE.	LONGITUDE.	FAHRENHEIT.
St. Augustine, Fla.	29° 48' N.	81° 29' W.	69.6°
Cairo, Egypt.	30° 2' N.	31° 20' E.	71.2°
Palatka, Fla.	29° 39' 40" N.	81° 40' W.	69.6°
Lisbon, Portugal	38° 42' N.	9° 6' W.	61.4°
Pinecastle, Fla.	28° 30' N.	81° 24' W.	72.6°
Delhi, India	28° 30' N.	80° 24' E.	64°
Sanford, Fla.	28° 48' 34" N.	61° 33' W.	68.7°
Naples, Italy	40° 1' N.	16° 20' E.	59.2°
Tampa, Fla.	27° 57' 30" N.	82° 28' E.	71.9°
Valencia, Spain	38° 20' N.	1° W.	72.3°
Key West, Fla.	24° 34' N.	81° 48' W.	76.5°
Jamaica	18° N.	77° W.	68°

MEAN COMPARATIVE HUMIDITY IN WINTER (FIVE MONTHS).

COUNTRIES.	NOV.	DEC.	JAN.	FEB.	MARCH.
	per cent.	per cent.	per cent.	per cent.	per cent.
Mentone and Cannes	71.8	74.2	72.0	70.7	72.4
Duluth, Minn.	74.0	72.1	70.7	72.3	72.4
Sanford, Fla.	76.2	76.5	77	75.7	72.5
Punta Rassa, Fla.	72.7	73.2	74.2	78.7	71.0
Boston, Mass.	66.0	61.6	68.6	68.2	65.5
Pinecastle, Fla.	73	74	75	74	72.3

It is right to add to this, that it does not include the rainy season of th summer months, which is the peculiar and inestimable advantage of the fruit grower, sparing him that onerous labor of hand irrigation, which burdens orange culture in every other country, except Florida, India, and New Zealand. From what has been given, the humidity or dryness of the Florida atmosphere compares favorably with the high plains of Minnesota, and the delightful climates of Mentone, Cannes and Nice. It justifies the dictum of Dr. Forry, U. S. A., that "the climate of this Land of Flowers is in no way inferior as a winter residence to the notable resorts of Italy, Madeira and Southern France." The learned scientist and archæologist, Dr. Brinton, of the same service, reporting on the arduous campaigning in the Everglades, compares the yearly mortality on the troops engaged, as but 27 per thousand, while in Texas it rose to 40, and in Lower Mississippi to 45 per thousand. A singular confirmation of this is in the reports of Capt. Menge, of Dredge Boat No. 1, engaged in the drainage of the Okechobee, and R. E. Rose, on like labor on the Upper Kissimmee. Having from twenty to forty laborers employed summer and winter, and up to their waists in the tepid water, not a case of malaria was reported in either gang. Something must be due in such striking examples, to physical hardihood and the genuine healthfulness of outdoor labor; but, with all reductions, it disposes of all reports of malaria arising from the Florida swamps. The climate has, in fact, been so beneficial in cases of asthma, bronchial and lung troubles as to give a curious justification to those earlier fables of the Elysian Fields, and fresh fountains of Living Water.

CHARLESTON AND SAVANNAH AND SAVANNAH, FLORIDA AND WESTERN RAILWAYS.

There is no city in the United States now so rich in incident, so distinct in character as the city of Charleston, S. C. As if the intermingling of Huguenot blood intensified the spirit that held it "base to plead for a fee;" and the names of Gadsden, Loundes, Hampton, keep up from age to age the heroic character of their city. Its early defence of Fort Moultrie is supplemented by its four years' resistance during the Civil war; as if the city was not destined to fall until the desperate cause it had originated had fallen. The American people now can afford to share in that pride which proved steadfast under trial, and quicken with sympathy that

"The earthquake's shock
Has left untouched the hoary rock;
The keystone of a land which still
Though fallen looks proudly from her hill."

It would be harder than the rock, however, looking down the famous Bay street, on the open bay, to see a cliff like the poet figures its prototype. The city lies bedded in swales of rice and corn between its Shaftesbury rivers, with the famous forts discovering their low, flat crowns in the dazzle of the open bay. An interesting study to the tourist is to observe the marks of the recent earthquake, still visible in the repaired walls of many a stately building; scars which shall as adequately mark the sympathy of the lately warring sections as the plugged holes of the cannon shot of the Swamp Angel. But still more admired and sought is the statue of the great Carolinian.

It is at this point the great transportation company of the South, the Plant System, takes charge of the tourist and makes all his ways the ways of pleasantness and all his paths of peace. The spirit of co-operation, characteristic of the age in its advantages more than its evils, has done nothing so strikingly beneficial as in systematizing travel. A man, even of middle age, can recall the ante-bellum days of the South, when migration was effected in private vehicles, or by a disconnected series of coaches and river lines, with scanty chances of railway, on strictly local lines. It was a period of vexation and confusion, defeating the most careful computations of time and opportunity. A cast shoe might be more expensive than a through ticket of to-day over a comfortable line. There were benefits of some kind, no doubt, in the simple, old fashioned methods; but it was a germinal period. The lonely horseback traveler, or the pioneer whose sole reliance was his team in the white-topped wagon, was picketing the way for the great railroad lines of the future. He carried unconsciously in the scow, the terminus and branches of some great railroad system. With the garden seed and fruits, he planted wayside stations whose seed would multiply some sixty fold, as the good book says.

But the transition from the stage line to the railway coach did not complete the system. Co-operation and competition had to adjust themselves; and, in that adjustment, perfect the Pullman sleeper, boudoir, buffet cars. In short, there was just that sort of drill and discipline in the growth which, in military affairs makes a prompt, efficient army of a heterogeneous mob. The tactical schools of railway affairs may not yet be perfect. The Inter-State Commerce bill affirms defects in definite relations; but the bill itself recognizes a comprehensive system, based on an intelligent business response to public demand. There have been errors in this reciprocal education of railroad managers and the public; but corporations, like individuals, are taught by their mistakes.

Necessarily, and from the diversity of intellect, there will be sensible differences in the conduct of a perfectly well-ordered system; but it is claimed for the Plant system, that its progressive development has been just that training necessary to a prudent and comprehensive discharge of its grave responsibilities. The traveler has that trust which springs from confidence in tried and experienced methods. A perfect discipline, a vigilant care of the comforts and convenience of its passengers is made a habit of the employees of the system. It is accepted by them that the traveler is dependent upon them, and courtesy and help is due, not merely that the service is paid for, but it is the generous obligation of their reciprocal relations. Under a like sense of obligation, all the service and appointments of the system are executed. The careful daily supervision of the roadbed, the attention to the machinery, the superior ease and comfort of the coaches, the solid elegance of all its equipments, are based upon the governing idea of a trust accepted, and to be discharged faithfully for the trust's sake.

This habitual method, associated with well-appointed carriage, buffet, boudoir coaches and Pullman sleepers, conveys such a delicious sense of ease and luxury, as to seem incompatible with travel. The elderly man contrasts it with his former experience of following the buffalo trails over the hills, and the apparently endless range of blue summits hanging for weeks on his flank; the camp when the clouds jarred with thunder and spouts of rain, the stiff mud locking the wheels; the hours of helpless sickness; the raw sand plains, and the lonely pine forest in which he seemed to sink like a stone into oceanic foliage; the dreary routine of it—all these come back to him with an incomprehensible sense of unrealism, in the vivid elegance about him. If some picturesque scene, some pleasing incident of that old journey comes back to him, it is associated with the heavy expense

HOOSIER SPRING, NEAR ALTAMONTE SPRINGS.

of time, money and physical energy. He can cross the continent at less cost of nerve force than it cost to go to the State capital.

Soft cushioned divans receive his body; a delicate luncheon is served at any hour; an airy "smoker" invites him to gossip with his fellow guests—they cannot be travelers. No, he is the guest of a hotel on wings. The grain of polished wood and nickel mountings, in arch and panel, and mirrors reflecting the flying scene without, strengthen the self deception. The quiet ardor of the strong, complicated, yet almost noiseless machine, with an imperceptible, bird-like vibration of its muscular phalanges, is a flight beyond capricious imagination. Towns, stations, villages, are flushed like par-

7

tridges, and go whirring out of sight, while the strong, deep bass of that monotone sings:

> "Yes, I am in the land of cotton,
> Cinnamon seed and a sandy bottom.
> Look away! Look away! Look away!
> Down in Dixie."

But the low, deep undertone of wheel and lever strikes a mightier harp than fabled Apollo's plectrum struck, as he flies by the Port Royal branch, the native home of the Sea-Island staple. Yes, this is the land of cotton, the home of secession; once so frightful a spectre, now grown romantic and fabulous. We flush more pretty towns, planted among live oaks. One finds one's self wondering over a life there, as if one shared it; and came down to business in an idle, sunny fashion, after breakfast; and had marketing to do for some one at home, and notes in bank to meet; how like ourself it all is after all.

Alternating from the wild salt-marsh, over wide pasture-like fields of lowland rice in brilliant green, and through startled villages, the hoarse throttle valve bellowing as if in sport, we cross the spidery spans of the iron bridge over the Savannah, and away through opening arcs of sunlight.

As we approach the city, a stout, handsome, smoothly-shaven gentleman of fifty, remarks to his companion, a slender, martial figure with white-trimmed mustache:

"There is a moral in that fable of Washington and his little hatchet. You've heard the story of course." "No," says the other with a twinkle in his dark-hazel eyes; at which improbable denial, an audible smile is provoked.

"I've half a notion telling it, to punish you; but hear the moral. The native American always has G. Washington's little hatchet in his hand, and goes about hacking down all the forest trees he meets. The excellence of Savannah lies in its having been severer in its discipline than the Grandfather of his country. It trounced its boy, so he learned to leave the forest trees standing; and in that lies the beauty of Savannah. It is a woods park. There is a green, shadowy coolness over it, that gives it a forest breath at all seasons." Every inclosed square is like a thyrsus; it has a park at its extremity. The residences are solid, noble structures, and surrounded by verdure, have a massive dignity. The architecture too is simple; is on plain lines, free of that straining for effect which in a cluster or block of houses, mars their grace. Forsythe Park is a woodland of twenty acres, set with rambling gravel walks; a cow path is the true line of beauty for a forest, and the splendor of magnolia, sycamore, among live oaks and pride of India, toss their blossoms down at the grotesque tritons spouting at them from a central fountain.

The statuary in these public parks is appropriate and graceful; one to the heroic Greene in Johnson Square; another to Pulaski, and the handsome Confederate monument of Carrara marble with typical statuary, to commemorate the heroic dead. Fountains, promenades, parks, invite the loiterer and make Savannah no less striking for the loveliness of its graceful belles, than the arts of sculpture, architecture and landscape gardening that constitute its peculiar and picturesque character.

8

There is an intuitive lesson in good breeding in the elegantly furnished parlor cars of the Savannah, Florida and Western. The coarsest nature is rebuked and refined by the studied elegance and purity of the designs. To be rude, boisterous or vulgar where the exquisite modeling and furniture are a constant lesson in harmony, is impossible. The habit of meeting and traveling together among them has had its influence on the lately hostile sections. Why not? What was it made Athens the most polished city of the world, but the graceful architecture of the Parthenon. Pheidias was as great a moral philosopher as Socrates or Plato; and this frequent meeting of the North and South in the midst of the elegances of travel, has equally made each to the other, the soft Southern drawl and crisp Northern syllable, seem the just tone of the polite world.

By mills and factories to Montgomery, where is the famous Southern regatta course. At Skidaway is the picnic grounds. Tybee Island, beyond the

HOTEL "ALTAMONTE," AT ALTAMONTE SPRINGS.

river's mouth, is the lighthouse and bathing ground. Bonaventura cemetery is a shell-road drive, and Thunderbolt river and its hostelries, a mile beyond. But why loiter over charming local resorts. The Savannah, Florida and Western connects with all winter resorts; the coy retreats and lovely by-places that fashion seeks when the dumb frost paints its Florida hamack on the window pane. One arm, *rem tetigit acu*, touches that junction of Flint river and the Chattahoochee, our English gentry marked as the point of departure to East and West Florida; the place too, of an abandoned fortification by the English, seized in 1816 by a fugitive slave, Garcias, with 3,000 stand of arms, two magazines and a battery of cannon. He held it, until Col. Clinch and gun-boat No. 154, at its fifth discharge of a hot shot in the

9

magazine, sent Garcias and his 300 bandits where the woodbine does not twine.

FLORIDA.

We have observed that Florida hangs to the stem of the states like an ear of Indian corn. Its sounds and silver rivers are the silk thereof; and that part which belts along the tier of states, a width of sixty miles, 366 miles east and west, is the spatha or sheath holding it to the culm. It is as deep north and south. A low swale extending to Brunswick, Ga., connects Oke-fenokee swamp to Apalachee hamacks, and the valley of the Suwannee. That is the physical division. Northwest of that diagonal is of one character, south, another very different.

The Savannah, Florida and Western Railway, to whose courtesy the read-er owes these shrewd observations of his, extends its arms, as we have

SCENE ON LAKE MINNEHAHA.

sketched, from the forks of the Chattahoochee to the ripraps of the St. Johns. But the spinal column, that which supports the frame, is the stem line up the St. Johns; or descending the Live Oak, Gainesville and Palatka branch, join the tourist crossing from St. Augustine to that point, proceed together into the very heart of orange production.

Waycross, the key point of this latter departure, is the distributing center of the Savannah, Florida and Western's various lines to all points of Florida. A short ride from this point brings us to

JACKSONVILLE,

the Initial City of Florida. Recent developments have been of ad-vantage to the picturesque beauty of the Initial City. Grand live oaks adorn broad, park-like thoroughfares. The city is substantially all water front, a Venezuela, or little Venice, stretching out on piles

10

PACKING ORANGES IN MINNEHAHA GROVE, MAYO.

11

into the broad bay, and leaning back on five parallel streets to the river, crossed by seven equally wide avenues to its many wharves. The river at the city's front has a width of 2,390 feet and a mean rise and fall of one foot. The city is twenty-four and a half miles by channel measurement from its mouth near Mayport, where rise and fall is 4.3 feet. The St. Johns is always clear, depositing no silt; but the deflection of the sea-coast line is such as to make a sort of pocket for a drift and wave bar. This constantly recasts the outer bar islands, rendering an historic preservation of noted sites improbable.

Among the beauties of the water front is the Yacht Club house, the gift of Mr. Astor, a beautiful building on piers, with locks and reservoirs for boats and sculls, and a handsome assembly room above; perhaps the most delightful resort for youthful recreation, on the Atlantic coast. The Everett, on Bay street, the *elite* boulevard of Jacksonville, looks from its broad verandas on the prismatic, picturesque river view, having reception for 500 guests. The Windsor is a favorite hotel among the many fastidious visitors, for the perfection of its cuisine and general appointments arranged for the entertainment of 400 guests. Across the way from this is the spacious and delightful caravanserai of the St. James, whose cool corridors and graceful porches invite the visitor to ease and sensuous enjoyment. These are provided with the usual complete equipment of modern fashion of elevators, electric lights and bells; and bands of music make the soft, tropical air throb with a delicious inspiration of rhythmic motion. The city has an active, intelligent, and independent press; a capable municipal government and police. The wharves are crowded with timber ships and cotton packets, and elegant Sound steamers. A trans-Atlantic line is projected for placing the South Florida tropical fruits in the European market, while the railway lines are fragrant with limes, lemons, citrons, oranges in season; and fresh vegetables, melons, peaches, apricots and grapes. Excursions are made to St. Georges Island at the mouth, and the supposed sites of the Spanish forts, beautiful in aisles of palmetto, shell beaches and white sand dunes. Capt. John H. McIntosh, engaged in the revolt against Spanish occupancy in 1812, entertained Aaron Burr for a short time on this island, St. Georges, and it has shared its hospitality with other noted semi-pirates and buccaneers in the lawless period of Florida history. The archæologist will find a triangular cinerary mound on Amelia, full of bones of great age mixed with pottery, commanding a wide view of the intervening salt marshes from its summit, set against the dark ground of Cumberland Island. The face of the bluff of Fernandina was made up of heaps of esculent oysters in separated valves, revealing an ancient custom of sea-side oyster dredging, extending over great periods. Green Cove Sulphur Springs is also another wonderful natural object worthy of inspection and within easy reach of Jacksonville.

ST. AUGUSTINE.

Any place at which strong men have sinned and suffered has a strange attraction for mankind, and St. Augustine, with its old fort, its relics, its mediæval streets, in contrast with the magnificent de Leon Hotel, with its complement of one thousand guests, unites in itself the elegant comfort of to-day and the mystery of Spanish legend. The luxurious coaches of the Jacksonville, Tampa and Key West Railway, invite the excursion; this new way of stepping on airy matting, resting on velvet cushions, and sleeping on caressing couches of poppy lidded slumber, while crossing scenes of savage warfare, heroic valor and brutal barbarity adds the last flavor to the dish. It is poor philosophy that fails to recognize the advantage. It is the small miseries that keep us from learning. Stanley on the Congo, or Greeley on the Arctic ice is handicapped with the daily grind of nerve, muscle and hunger ache; but the philosopher following in a buffet saloon car, studies their heroics with a divine impartiality. It is evident that a great many heroic characters have been lost to history just for the lack of these conveniences. A buggy brigade would find ample volunteers, and a Pullman sleeper and buffet saloon car would enlist whole nations—in transport. It is apparent, from the window of the smoker, that poor old Quixotic Ponce de Leon was all wrong in that Baptist theory. Why wish to be young? He had been that once. The whole spirit of modern life is to be something else; something that you were not, and quite new. The idea of taking up with the cold victuals of yesterday. Pah! And smelled so, Horatio?

But in the narrow courts of St. Augustine one does get a little flavor of the antique, as if one had lived it once, and was glad to have it over. It is pleasant enough as a memory, as the heroics of a legend. There was something in the gallant old marquis after all. We can trace the pretty pomegranates; the orange and palm to the seed; but what planted yon grand palace with its fittings for a thousand royal guests? Certainly, it was our old friend Ponce. But for him the hotel would be a myth instead of the fountain; and St. Augustine can not spare the famous de Leon Hotel, with its noble outlooks, grand galleries and grand orchestral bands, throbbing like the pulses of the outer sea.

THE PEOPLE'S LINE, JACKSONVILLE, TAMPA AND KEY WEST RAILWAY.

—JACKSONVILLE TO SANFORD.—

The South Florida, and those branches treated of, may be regarded as local to Sanford and its environment. It includes that portion of the road which went into operation June 1, 1880.

But from that the road rapidly pushed its connections, opening up the country as it progressed, and strengthening its associations at all important points. At that time and later, the conditions of travel on the St. Johns river were exceedingly disagreeable. Controlled by a monopoly, or contested by individuals or companies without sufficient capital to command public confidence, the demand for a reformation was immediate and pressing. It led to the institution of the People's Line, the name itself expressing a protest against monopoly, which entering definitely into the Plant Investment system, became an assurance to the public of good faith, honorable dealing, and what is more, a swift and comforable passage and direct rail connections. It is no part of this itinerary to find fault or censure rival lines. It is to their interest to make travel pleasant, but an isolated part is free to dump the traveler at its terminus, leaving him to the mercies of stevedores and impertinent solicitors. All that was reformed by the establishment of the People's Line. A common responsibility and mutual dependence made the care of the traveler entrusted to one the business responsibility of the other. A

13

line of handsome, well-equipped steamers especially adapted to run on the St. Johns, rapid, safe, finished in elegant state rooms, was officered by gentlemen of experience and trust—rather better than the steamboat songs had it :

> " Push along de gang plank, gwine down de river.
> Boat he git behin' time, t'ought it was her liver.
> Pitch, tar and turpentine; gettin' late and later,
> Better give de engine Simms's regulator."

A journey up the St. Johns is full of beauty, rife with historic associations, and trial and endeavor of Northern men seeking health and a home during that earlier recent period which is indeed the heroic age of South Florida. But the development is too rapid and sanguine for water travel. The spirited and enterprising Jacksonville, Tampa and Key West line took the short, direct course down the St. Johns River; and became a valuable and necessary co-adjutant of the South Florida, and the Plant Investment system.

THE GARDENS OF THE HESPERIDES.

The pioneer of Orange who points out to his Northern visitor his wide orange grove stretching along the lake front in vain claims the discovery of this fruitful country. The archæologist exhuming relics confirms the

THE "SEMINOLE," WINTER PARK.

historian. De Soto, in his letter to the Municipal Council, alleges that " Such abundant return rewarded their (the natives') light toil, the largest army could be supported without exhausting the resources of the land;" and Laudonniere locates the tribes by name after his ascent of the St. Johns, so that we can define the region as including the valley of that river, and across to Mucoso, a point near Tampa, mentioned by De Soto's narrative. It includes Orange and parts of Polk, Hillsborough, Sumter, Hernando. The itinerary of the Incas narrative carries De Soto to Ichipuchisassa, lat. 28 deg. 5 min., long. 82 deg. from which the course was twenty leagues north and northeast. This would follow the old trail by Fort Davenport and Lake Conway,

14

or farther west among the shell heaps of Lake Apopka. These interesting regions are opened to travel by the South Florida Railroad, and the mounds are discovered all along the route. One of the most interesting of these was at Mount Royal, already referred to, at the southern extremity of Lake George. It was the home of Olata, king of the Akuera, in 1564. It is now the golden gate to the famous Gardens of the Hesperides in Orange, and

"Groves whose rich trees wept odorous gums and balm,
Others whose fruit, burnished with golden rind,
Hung amiable, Hesperian fable true
If true here only, and of delicious taste."

THE SOUTH FLORIDA RAILROAD.

While the South Florida Railroad is a part of the grand international system of the Plant Investment Company, whose highways of steel rail and ocean steamer knit together the business and social relations of cities, states and foreign countries, it is none the less a distinct integer, having an

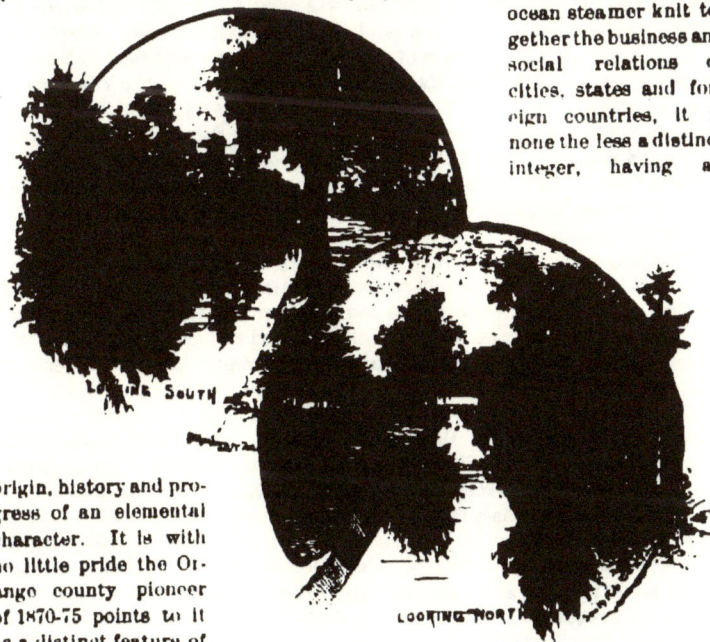

LOOKING SOUTH

LOOKING NORTH

CANAL BETWEEN LAKES OSCEOLA AND VIRGINIA,
WINTER PARK.

origin, history and progress of an elemental character. It is with no little pride the Orange county pioneer of 1870-75 points to it as a distinct feature of that strong, courageous business sense that cleared the forest and planted the orange. It was no bonanza of an oil strike; no railroad wrung from the public purse brought about the settlement of Orange. The pioneer knew he must face ten years of patient endurance for the tree to mature, if it ever did mature; and the South Florida, the first railroad south of lat. 29 deg. north, founded by the same men, engineered, officered, conducted on the same solid business principles of doing the work honestly, correctly, carefully, is as sound to the core as the substantial groves about it.

15

In 1877-8 the young groves not in bearing were full of promise. Orange culture was a pronounced success. Dr. C. C. Haskell, Mr. B. R. Swoope, Mr. Jas. E. Ingraham, Mr. E. W. Henck and others projected the railroad connecting the county site at Orlando with the port of Sanford. Articles of incorporation were made and a charter granted June, 1879, with a capital of $120,000 for a railroad connecting the St. Johns at Sanford with the Gulf coast. Surveys began Nov. 10, 1879, and Jan. 10, 1880, Gen. Grant, then visiting the county, threw out the first ceremonial spadeful. As if to complete the moral union Messrs. Halsted, E. B. Haskell and Mr. R. M. Pulsifer, of the Boston *Herald*, became interested and provided the most of the capital. It was significant of a sound union between the North and South, contradicting the proscriptions of the period. The road was open for freight and travel to Orlando by Dec. 1, 1880. It was a careful, thrifty, economic road, adapted to the limited but growing business of the county. It was extended to Kissimmee and opened for business March, 1882, and, entering into the Plant syndicate, was pressed through to Tampa, and opened to travel Feb., 1884. In the following years it extended branches to Pemberton's Ferry, connecting with the Florida Southern, and to Bartow, in Polk, connecting with the same line to Punta Gorda. Each step has been based upon sound business principles. The original narrow gauge was continued until the interests of its connections required the standard.

This progressive development, neither sluggish nor immature, but always competent to the demand, has characterized the general management. It has adopted every comfort, convenience and safeguard for travel as it appeared. The track is 40-pound steel rails, soundly ballasted and under constant supervision, a caution that has so far in its experience exempted the road from loss of life by any traveler in its coaches. Wharton's improved safety switches, and patent boxes avoiding annoyance by smoke, are among the ordinary precautions. It has provided the elegant buffet boudoir parlor coaches and patent Pullman sleeperr. While it has thus kept pace with modern improvements, this example of a road originated and conducted by energetic young men of Orange county, is a lesson of example to our young business men of the South, and an assurance to travel of experienced, careful management. It is believed there is no line covering a like extent, or brought in contact with so novel physical and business complications, that can show as uniformly pleasant and successful record. Its popularity is by no means limited to the local travel, for it ranks among the soundest, safest managed lines on the continent.

ORANGE COUNTY.

This garden county, recently subdivided by a line on the north boundary of Township 25, forming the northern base of the new county of Osceola, is in form a right angled triangle, having its vertex lat. 29 deg., 15 min., T. 14, R. xxvii, its western perpendicular deflected to enclose the Eastern Apopka Lake basins and the St. Johns on the east. The Ocklawaha and St. Johns flow north from opposite sides bounding it, while the Kissimmee from its reservoir lake flows south. In or near the center, from the summit level, Lake Conway, 112 feet above tide-water, a number of streams flow to all points, dividing the area into terraces. In the enclosed area are eight hundred lake basins, small and great, and a number of mineral springs. The natural and mechanical distributing center to these various points of interest is the original base of the South Florida Railroad at Sanford.

SANFORD.

Sanford is on the west bank of lake Monroe, 125 miles south of Jacksonville. It first appears in history as occupied by the left wing of the Indian army in 1837, under Micanopy and Osceola in their attack on Fort Mellon, the site of an Indian village. The American force was under Colonels Fanning and Harney, and among the names distinguished in the engagement was one Lieut. Thomas, who survived, to save the right wing of Gen. Rosecrans's army at Chicamauga. Among the slain was Capt. Mellon, of the 2d Artillery, and the site was called after him Fort Mellon. Under the armed occupation act, H. A. Crane took up the greater section, including Mellonville, and A. J. Vaughn that of Fort Reid, two miles south on the highlands. Dr. Sidney Speer set out the Speer Grove of sour stumps, a few years later, and the Beck and Hughey Groves near Sanford were planted in 1850. Supplies were brought by row-boats from Palatka until 1865, when Messrs. Doyle & Brantley

SCENE ON LAKE CONCORD, ORLANDO.

opened a warehouse. In 1868 Dr. L. U. Moore was made postmaster, and the next year, 1869-70, Hon. W. M. Randolph built the Orange House at Fort Reid.

The present city of Sanford was originally a Spanish grant to P. R. Young, for the secretary of the Spanish Governor, Juan Entralgo, who selling to Moree Levy, the matter fell in Chancery and was purchased by Gen. Jos. Finnegan, general of the Confederate forces at Olustee. Gen. Finnegan sold to Gov. Sanford, ex-Minister to Belgium, an accomplished student of tropical growth in the gardens of Italy.

The body lies on a square, conformable to the shores of Lake Monroe, which have an alignment north northeast, crossing the squares of the townships. The west bank of the St. Johns, south of Hawkinsville to Wilson's Ferry, at the mouth, is a low palmetto swamp. The lake shore, however, rises fourteen feet in a terrace which slopes upward in a broad terrapin back on which the city stands, losenged in wide, airy streets. The water front, except the horticultural park in front of the Sanford House, is unimproved. The main thoroughfare, for a mile of broad airy perspective, is handsomely built up in business blocks, to which additions are in construction at every hundred yards. Parallel streets, lined with residences and pretty flowering courts, and espaliers clustered with vines, are crossed by wide avenues descending to the water front. The streets are handsomely lighted and aqueducts draw veins of sparkling water from the cool hills beyond. There is a fine Episcopal church with stained glass windows and an interior finish of great elegance. The Presbyterians and Methodists have equally stylish houses of worship, and about them, as about the dwellings, is the peculiar lightness and airy freshness proper to the open air life of the tropics. One is struck by the excess of business houses, but this is readily explained by the character of the city. It is the Damascus, or the Jacksonville of South Florida. At this point the South Florida Railroad, gathering to it the various tributary branches is the recipient and exponent of the great Plant Investment system. An active and liberal promoter of every enterprise of public interest, it studies the wants and conveniences of the surrounding country, and makes a center of business around it. In addition to its Sanford and Indian river lines and branches, the Jacksonville, Tampa and Key West, the Atlantic Coast, St. Johns and Indian river, and the Sanford and Lake Eustis Railways contribute. The De Bary and the popular People's Line to Jacksonville, and Hart & Smith's packets to Rockledge and Upper St. Johns add to the general business activity. An hourly ferry to Enterprise connects the local interests of Orange and Volusia counties. Gov. Sanford, some years ago, transferred his growing interests at this point to an Anglo-American company, the agency for which is in the hands of Mr. F. H. Rand, a very able and experienced trustee, entirely familiar with the interests of the city and its surroundings.

But nourished by these arteries of her commerce, Sanford has other attractions to give the city the appearance of a public bazaar or watering-place, or both. She sits among her palms, the most distinctly oriental in appearance of South Florida cities. Its typical foliage is redolent of old Arabic tale and mythological fable, and this charm of her picture is infinitely improved by the situation on the broad bosom of Lake Monroe. At all hours beautiful, whether holding the shadows of her yachts and wherries, and the double of her long-legged wharves in the still river's reflections, or when at night the incoming steamer, itself a flying constellation of starry lights, sees rise from the water a phantom-like city, crossed and losenged by its line of lights, recalling the mediæval fable of the kingdom of Prester John. The beautiful hotel, glancing in serried rows of burners, makes a golden background for the tall tufted topped palms ; and the band plays, the music throbs and mellows over the water, and we seem to be sailing on the calm Bendemeer. Sweeter still is that cool fresh dawn when

> " The moon is low in the sky
> And a sweet south wind is blowing,
> Where the bergamot blossoms breathe and die
> In the orchard's scented snowing;
> But the stars are few and scattered lie
> Where the sinking moon is going."

18

Seen among its palm groves in that pure, pearly light of dawn Sanford is like a picture under glass. A European city of half its natural beauty would ravish the poets.

But sketching its privileges we have yet to recall what makes it—the back country whose production is poured into her lap. The Spear grove, Beck grove, Hughey grove, the Randolph, Whitner, Belair and twenty other great ten, twenty, hundred acre parks of bearing orange trees. To see these in their beauty one must take a buggy and follow the picturesque old Fort Mellon-road among the groves and gardens of a prior generation; or following the line of the Indian River branch to Jesup, see the strange contrasts of bare piney woods, dense green hamack, and miles of orange groves.

Coming out of the hamack, proud of its blue flags, we ascend the crest of a park-like forest on the old Fort road; and passing between tall picket fences, over which hangs the dark varnished green of the orange, grove after grove, we come to old Fort Reid. After the battle of Mellonville, Feb. 8, 1837,

LAKE EOLA, ORLANDO, FROM ARMORY BUILDING.

Lieut. Col. Harney completed the hasty fortifications and posted a force at Fort Mellon. But as the season advanced, apprehensive of malaria from the surrounding swamps, he built and fortified a position two miles out on the cool hills, beside the old Tampa trail. The Orange House, now the residence of Mr. B. M. Robinson, stands on the old site, surrounded by a noble orange grove. The building was erected in 1870 and was the first hotel south of Palatka. The present grove was set out for Hon. W. M. Randolph. It still preserves that reputation of pure air and hygienic advantage which caused its selection just half a century ago, by Lieut. Col. Harney and the Medical Staff of the U. S. Second Dragoons. No spectacle could be more striking than the view from the broad upper verandas of this quaint old inn, now a gentleman's home. As far as the eye can reach is that scene of pine forest, with strong illumination of grand squares of stately groves standing out on the tawny green background, and against the pearly iridescent Florida sky line.

A mile beyond we come on the beautiful basins of Golden, Onoro, and Silver Lake. On Lake Onoro is the residence and grove of Rev. Lyman Phelps, a place of singular loveliness, to which the skill and scholarship of an accomplished planter has added an herbarium of tropical fruits. The illustration gives some ideal of this picturesque spot, but it lacks color, the delicate penciling of Florida atmosphere; orange, fig, pomegranate, bergamot.

THE BERGAMOT.

" We had no other gifts to give
But just one withering flower:
We had no other lives to live,
But just that sweet half hour:
So small, so sweet, its freight of musk,
Made fragrant all life's after dusk.

" For this the summer toiled and spun,
With fairy fingers silken shot,
Till moonlight's milky threads were run
In the scented creamy bergamot:
That gave one dear remembered hour
The fragrance of the orange flower."

While the immediate vicinity of Sanford delights in many a paradise, there is none more choice and various in its charm than this. These three lakes are handsomely set in groves and picturesque forest scenery, making the Onoro vicinage an attractive summer-like home.

The site of the old fort is also the center of a cluster of groves surrounding a station on the Sanford and Indian River Railroad, which here connects with the St. Johns on Lake Jesup. The neighborhood is full of a rustic prettiness, and simple country churches, free of the vain effort to erect a granite Gothic out of light pine espaliers. It is somehow "Sweet Auburn, loveliest village of the plain." One pictures to one's self a vision of the old South; its sweet, gentle aristocratic tone, into which the Northern element has entered and harmonized, forming a delightful society of peculiar inoffensive fastidiousness, and gentle morality. A mile or two beyond is a charming pavilion like a round summer house, and the usual platform of a station. It is Rutledge.

Like Fort Reid, but more recent and rural. No village and square of shops breaks the park-like distances; but there are white picket fences and avenues leading to a low-roofed Southern cottage, that seems to have broadened its eaves into a farm house. The orange groves reach out around it, and mask the stabling and conservatory. Well dressed ladies wait at the station, and there is the low voiced, pleasant murmur of feminine laughter, that somehow quickens attention. There are glimpses of roofs in the distances, and the dark green even line of groves beyond the columnal pines; and occasionally an opening shows the villas and country seats of gentlemen more completely. But we plunge into the raw woods again, through pine and oak scrub and fire bitten swales, and green tongues of cypress swamp protruding into them. Then, as if by a coup de théatre, we glance through

INTERIOR VIEW OF SOUTH FLORIDA EXPOSITION, FEB. 15TH, 1887.

coulisses of arborage, tall white picket fences and miles on miles of orange groves, in superb order, and mastership of wealth—the grand Whitner and Foster groves. We dip by younger trees, looking sparse by contrast; lean saw palmetto and purpling puddles by the wayside, and the swales of green hamack skirmish nearer the line; and nearer, on it, over it, covering and inclosing it like a roof. We are going through a dark evergreen tunnel. At each side, solid as a wall, the thick black-green impenetrable mass of foliage rises. It is like a wall, as if blasted out of the solid, dense block of granite—pomegranate, of course, but it is not that, and it is hard to describe. Every tree, and they are thick as an army in column, rank in rank, crowded shoulder to shoulder, breast to back. A huge cypress, six feet through, bulges up out of the olive brown water; a green, snake-like creeper grapples it in rising spirals, throwing out tendrils leafing lazily a yard apart. Over that again is a mass of jasmine, greenbriar, liane, bignonia, ananas, mosses, air plants, fungoids, a strangle of vegetation on a single tree. But the trees are densely crowded. Cypress, bay, cedar, magnolia, live oak, water oak, willow, water maple, white oak, and reeds, rushes, butomas, vallianeria, sarracenia, choking, scrambling, blackening from the copper-brown pools below to the lofty pencilled foliage above. But there are gaps; hollows in the solidity like natural caves, on which the grass is long, thick and fine, and the ground spongy with moisture, and again the jungle overflows the road, solid, massive as ever. One begins to recognize a task of engineering. Dynamite will do no good here; mechanism is at fault, as it is apt to be combating organic nature. That black, venomous looking mass must be fought hand to hand, with axe, pick and spike.

We skip out into a flat of smoky pools, damp green patches and into the pines, bearing an undergrowth of lyrate leafed oak. We come to recognize it. After the sawmill has skinned the pine wood, the swamp white oak rushes up to take its place; fills the gaps as fast as opened. The white oak means a saw mill, houses, fences, gardens, groves hard by. We pass a sour jungle of gall berries, of scrub palmetto, the spurs of Lake Jesup skirmishing up to the roadside in sharp re-entering curves. The throttle valve takes a fit; it yells a deep bass horror; it is terribly nervous, and it has a hoarse, horrible cold. But it bellows as if in frightful terror and dismay. Are we about to tumble over the edge of the world? We peep cautiously out. Pshaw! a half dozen lean, bone-picked cows, ashamed to be small as a mutton, but pert, bless you, tossing their lean whips of tails, and stopping to shake their dry, horny heads as if they meant something.

A quiet old fashioned country road pokes out in a bo-peep fashion and goes swaggering across the rails, to hide in the "bay head" beyond. As the eye turns from following, it flushes a rambling rail fence and raw clearing, and then a cabbage patch; respectable burgher-like cabbage too, broad in the girth, solid in the base; then the blank end of a church and belfry, neat offices, cottages. A street comes lilting down the hillside from a quite "sightly," i. e. picturesque dwelling on its crown. It is peaked, porticoed in a feather of vines and foliage, and orange groves, kitchen gardens, stabling. Why, yes, it is a town—Oviedo.

There is a red warehouse, a handsome depot in the neat South Florida

Railroad style; a water tank on stilts, a switch, and stores and warehouses and barrels of fertilizers, and crates of vegetables for shipment. It is two miles south of Lake Jesup, a fish-shaped lake with a heterocercal tail back and abdominal fin on section line of 13-18, of T. 20, R. xxxi, six miles south and east of Sanford, nine feet above tide-water, set in a limestone basin pregnant with sulphur, chalybeate and mineral springs. The southwestern extremity is surrounded by grand groves, truck gardens and villa farms at Lake Jesup City, Lake Charm, Oviedo and Tuskawilla. A beautiful borderland is

THE "TROPICAL," KISSIMMEE.

situated a little southwest of the center, composed of natural phosphated guano. It contains some forty acres, including a grove of cabbage palmetto.

A switch from Oviedo, a mile west, crossing low slants skirted by wire fences, young groves scant of foliage from excessive pruning, perhaps, comes on a neat Norman church, a large, square, red warehouse on the left and a farm house and grove on the slope above and beyond. A low swale interrupts the slope, and across the track and to the right the eye rests with pleasing content on Lake Charm. It is in the middle of a shallow swale whose smooth incline is covered with a soft green sward set in beautiful live oaks. It forms, including the depression proper to its continents, several hundred acres, formed into a sort of amphitheatre about the lake. A large, delightfully home-looking and hospitable residence, closed in with green blinds, stands

23

near the station under a grove of live oaks, water oaks and chinqua pine, at good spaces between. The basin is perfectly round in that shallow saucer-like depression, and picturesque villas, vine covered cottages in shrubbery, orange grove and vineyard, completely encircle the reservoir, discovering a landscape of consummate beauty, and like a fancy sketch. It is the seat of the Clifton Springs, first opened to observation by Dr. Henry Foster, of Clifton Springs, N. Y., and subsequently graced by the settlement of Rev. J. B. West, of Nashville, Tenn.; Maxwell & Bro., Geneva, N. Y.; Dr. J. S. Jewel, Chicago, Ill.; Hon. L. S. Kilham, Rochester, N. Y.; George Couch, Esq., Minneapolis, Minn.; William Deering, Esq., Chicago; Rev. J. H. Owens, Mass.; Dr. Dodson, Wisconsin; Hon. J. F. Allison. Ill. East and south of Sanford are the groves and settlements of Belair, New Upsala, Twin Lakes and many others, whose fruitfulness and scenery are of like character.

SOUTH FLORIDA RAILROAD AND ITS BRANCHES.

On leaving the station at Sanford, the grade rises gradually, as the traveler from the window of his boudoir saloon looks on the sliding panorama. The low, hoarse music that the wheel whispers to the rails begins. Skirting patches of sour-looking verdure, speaking of hardpan, and raw sulphur wrung from the vegetation. Shallow pools glance by and the lyrate leafed oak begins to show among the slender pines on the low, tumid ground. Another generation will find the white oak to succeed the pine that so long usurped the soil.

The ground tilts and shifts by low inclination, but the ascent soon becomes evident. This scenery is not like that covered on our road to Lake Jesup. Crystal Lake is not fortified in the dense hamacks of Lake Jesup. The water comes frankly up to a shelving beach, and there is a boat house on the right, and a young grove coming down to it and reaching out over the hills. We appear to cross a natural embankment that divides it from Lake Mary, but on the west its arm makes a grand river-like bend in the offing. The road parts the young groves, but as we slide south, the pine wood reopens in double distances. A gentle slope resembles the vanishing point; but while the eye is reconciled to it, suddenly a blue distance of forest crosses the low sky line and we feel cheated. A few miles further by this ascending grade and we are at Longwood.

This is a commanding point between the southern extremity of Lake Jesup, and the nest of mineral springs that forms the main source of the Wekiva. Over these depressions a broad flattened carapace of clay lies like a saddle, with one stirrup at Clifton Springs on Lake Charm and the other on the Wekiva. A large, handsome hotel, for the accommodation of fifty or sixty guests, faces the plaza, laid off in squares for a lawn of tropical fruits. The town is adorned by a beautiful church, and school building, besides a number of business houses. The most important industry of the vicinity is the mill machinery for cutting and moulding the fine woods of the adjacent country. These include the curled pine, the cypress, red cedar, *Cedralia odorata* and the red bay. The first has a marvelously graceful grain, which under polish is one of the most beautiful woods for panelling. The bay, or Florida mahogany, is another delicately fine grained wood whose sinuous curves and exquisite shading rival mahogany. These trees are found in the

24

hamacks and bays adjacent to the Longwood Mill, and an intelligent conception and execution of the purpose of the plant cannot fail to develop an important interest.

Resuming our journey we soon reach the station at Altamont Springs; a handsome omnibus coach and tramway receives the guest, and he is carried swiftly and smoothly out to this charming retreat. A large square building with broad south style veranda opening on a bright flowered plaza welcomes the tourist. There is a stately providence in its outlook, a promise of luxury and thoughtful provision in its many-windowed front, or double front, for it faces many ways. It stands in the pine forests, the " piney woods " of the South, whose pungent aromatic air, breathing of ambergris and spice, science and experience unite in pronouncing wholesome.

LAKE ALFRED, BARTOW JUNCTION.

Those broad valved chambers invite the cool freshness of the scented air to a hundred and twenty-five guests, and the cuisine studies the fastidious palate of bon vivant and invalid. The Altamonte Hotel is a sweet place to be tired and hungry in; or to find and feed an appetite for a too delicate digestion. Elevators, electric bells, all the smooth ingenuity by which the modern mode makes service a matter of volition is adopted here. Among the natural elements to this is the pure water from Altamonte Spring. It is with pride that we assert that this is not the Fountain of Youth. The entire failure of that particular spring to put in an appearance justifies a sound distrust of its

25

moral character; but the analysis of the water of the Altamonte Spring shows that it honestly is what it assumes to be, a water of singular purity and freshness, containing in 10,000 parts, 15 inorganic matter, 10 organic, 25 residue, with traces of chlorides and sulphate of lime. Three and a half miles west of Altamonte are Hoosier and Shepherd Springs. It is a wild, rolling country of parks and groves, crossed by the old country road. The first bulges up a huge boiling volume of pure, cold sulphur water, strongly impregnated with magnesia and other salines found peculiarly efficacious in rheumatic complaints. Shepherd Spring stands in a jungle, a dark pool of peculiarly clear water, that looks golden in the light, and saturated with iron and sulphur, the medical qualities of which are an Indian tradition. It was the custom of the medicine men in using for healing purposes to first breathe upon it, invoking the aid of the Great Spirit. Cooacoochee, the true hero of the Florida war, said that when the spirit of his twin sister came to him from the land of souls, she offered him a cup of pure water which she said came from the spring of the Great Spirit, " and if I should drink of it I should return and live with her forever."

But we have not suggested what is the great beauty of Altamonte Springs. It is the cluster of lakes surrounding the hotel. Orienta, in front, reaches into the forest in grand river-like bends, losing itself in possible remote distances. On the other side is the bright pool of Adelaide, on the borders of which a light wooden pavilion stands over its own reflection. The surrounding hills, crowned with handsome villas in bronze and yellow facings, come down from their orange orchards on smooth wooded slopes. The lawns are set in shrubbery and espaliers, with trailing vines and vases full of flowering plants. The perspective is crossed with the low farm fences and orange groves, and beyond, the mystery of cedar knolls and lakes in cultivated fields.

At Mary's there is an increment of groves on the line; a pretty lake bordered with golden canopies adjoins the old mill site, and a factory. Across the sunny haze is a line of picket fences, groups of orange trees looking over them. A narrow gauge road connects with the main stem and transfers the tourist to the shadowy Forest City vicinage These people persist in styling their villa homes cities, but it a gracious providence that they are not. The *rus in urbe* is decidely more *rus* than *urbe*, and all the prettier for it. Forest City is thus a stretch of pretty villas, groves and truck gardens arranged along a winding cluster of lakes in the forest, It displays in architecture and floriculture those traits by which South Florida is gradually assuming the appearance of Italy; not in climate alone, but in the external habits of living that belong to a wealthy rural province.

THE MAIN LINE.

There are artificial stoneworks at Mayo, on the main line, from which we resume our excursion after a jaunt to Forest City, and cottages and young groves, looking awkward as squab pigeons, excess of leg and scant of feather. Far reaches of woodland with mottes of green hamack on them. A grassy pool and quiet country road coming in by young groves. The ground swells and undulates, breaking the perspective again into double distances. There are swales and hamacks, and patches of spruce, setting its finely divided foliage against the sky. A picturesque church points its spire upward;

and the groves thicken and cluster; are thicker and more of them, greening the low horizon with bright, dark foliage. Cottage, picket and paling fences and the crowded roofs of a pretty little city. As the pace slackens, and that huge Roc, the engine, begins Sinbad like, to stoop to one of its nests, we pass a pool that has a story, and an unromantic name—It is John's Hole, in Maitland. It is a very pretty little Bethesda, and the Angel of Sal Soda, or Sal Ammoniac might well stir it a little. It is nearly round, a bright pool of some twenty to forty acres, having a low flare edge. Like many Orange county pools, it has a trick of its own. It has a shallow shelving border of still green confervæ, twenty or thirty feet out; but then it drops to twenty or more feet of depth. One observes odd little crosses, like finger boards, at the sides. One can read on the side facing the bank the admonition: "Don't shoot the alligators," but it requires craning a good deal to read the reverse side, to the saurians: "Don't bite the bathers," but this is not the story.

THE LEGEND OF JOHN'S HOLE.

In the days of the pro-consulships there lived a few miles below Orlando, on Lake Conway, a family whose mother called its head John. This mother was a thrifty housewife indeed, and kept herself and children by raising poultry, while John fished, hunted and jobbed out, doing chores of clearing and plowing after he had begged and planted his sweet potato sets—Hyti patch. The chickens enjoyed this happy go-lucky o utdoor life quite as much as John, and increased and multiplied mightily and were fat and firm of flesh and oily of feather. When they reached that succulent age when they may be expected to dine out like Polonius behind the arras, Mrs. John gathered them into coops, which John bound with rawhide to the wagon-bed and hitched to his ox team, to carry them to the Orange House, at Fort Reid. In those days there was no house north of Orlando to Fort Reid, and wayfarers nooned and roasted a cow's rib or venison chop on a stick over the coals, while the oxen fed and strayed at this round pool. It was late in the spring chicken season, the way was hot and dusty, and by the time John and his steers reached this oasis they were droughty and tired. He drove down the gentle slope, the tired steers plucking up at the sight of water, and shambling into a clumsy trot into the water. John woa'd and woa-hawed, at the pitch of his compass and tugged vainly at the guide rope on their horns. It was no use. The beasts wanted water, water down their hot throats and on their hot flanks. John yelled, and cracked his long thonged, short-handled cow whip, and woa-hawed (A Southern ox driver says Woa-haw when a Northern driver says Gee-up; a sectional point for philology) but to no purpose. John gave the rebel yell; the chickens cackled, and the stubborn yoke plunged on. Plunged on and over the steep, deceptive brink into deep water, drowning themselves and the chickens, poor John barely escaping with the loss of team, freight and wagon. Ever after in memory of his misfortune it was called John's Hole.

Even in those days Maitland (pronounced Metlan') branch was renowned for the picturesque beauty of its landscape. A chain of lovely lakes from Ivanhoe, in Orlando, Rowena, Virginia, Berry, Mizell, Osceola, Maitland and Howells, form a chain falling away into Howell's Creek that empties into

Lake Jesup. On the other side of the railroad, south of Lake Orienta, T. 21, S. of R. xxix, E., at the cross sections of 13, 14, 25, 26, is Spring Lake; Faith, Hope and Charity extending up to the vicinity of Orlando, which drain off into the east branch of the Wekiva, emptying into the St. Johns. We are nearing the crest of the country from which the water flows to every point of the compass. The old county roads, by a simple law of physical economy, followed these water courses generally to Lake Jesup and Wilson's Landing, and the older groves are collected upon them, partially removed from the main stem, the spinal column of the South Florida Railroad, that gives it frame and firmness. But from the cars the deep, rich magnificence of the Maitland groves is visible.

We draw up at a new, handsome depot in a style of architecture to suit the handsome villas sunk in dense groves of orange and shrubbery. The walks, by residences with wide open lawns in the cool of forest trees, and parterres of flowers, are very inviting. There is the Episcopal Church, Methodist Church and its handsome parsonage. Beautiful drives that descend to rustic bridges overhung by live oak and magnolia, and sloping lawns rich in orange, lime and lemon. A beautiful park has been laid out within the corporate limits, just north of Maitland branch, a picturesque point, and John's pool is set like a jewel at the intersection of four broad main highways, over whose white picket fence border the clustered orange hangs in rich gold and green. The town was first laid out by Major M. R. Marks and Mr. George Packwood, the town hall was built, and Judge McBrayer, of Kentucky, was followed by a number of refined and cultivated families, indulging in elegant respectabilities. Gen. Ivison, Mr. Patton and some others settled in the vicinity, and the development of Mr. Beasley's grove, of Kentucky, who had planted on Maitland branch in the early seventies, was followed by the maturing of many others. A large, elegant and roomy hotel was established at the Park House, which has steadily kept its place and popularity among the families of solid men from the West and South, having easy accomodations for fifty guests.

It will be readily understood that in ascending the divide between miles of orange groves, but scantily parted by pine forest and mottes of lyrate leafed oak, the stations rather mark artificial municipal than real divisions. There are dense coppices in drapery of long gray moss; umbrageous woods, and round grassy pools interrupting the background of pine forest. Swales of dark green meadows, oak groves and young orange groves again and again deepening into mature orange orchards in the magnificence of dark varnished leaf, and we roll into an open plaza and draw up at a handsome depot. It is Winter Park.

The prospect is squared into warehouses, business houses, smith and wagon factories, grocery and general merchandise, the railroad combing the town apart, male fashion, with the hair on one side. It is situated on the boss of the plateau lying between Lakes Killarney and Osceola, T. 21, S. of R. xxix and xxx, sections 13 and 7 respectively; but its skirts wave wide and flowing from Maitland to Orlando, being a rather high strung, pretentious, aristocratic neighborhood, affecting exclusive Northern habit and fashion of life. It is very sweet and pleasant in its ways, and one has a sincere wish all Northern modes were like it. It is conducted by a company of wealthy stock owners, consisting of Franklin Fairbanks, Esq., St. Johnsbury. Vt., president; J. F. Welborne. Esq., Winter Park, Fla., vice-president; William C. Comstock, Chicago, Ill., treasurer; A. W. Rollins, Chicago, auditor; F. B. Knowles, C. H. Hutchins, Worcester, Mass.; Peleg Peckham, St. Louis, Mo., and J. S. Capon, Winter Park, secretary. Among the most desirable accomplishments of this intelligent body of capitalists is the erection of a hotel really worthy of the climate and themselves. It is arranged for the accommodation of four hundred guests; it is heated throughout by steam and lighted by gas, and arranged with elevator, electric bells, fire alarm. suadaria, or steam baths, and hot and cold baths. approved fire protection and escape and good drainage. The vegetables are fresh from the

EAGLE LAKE, EAGLE LAKE STATION.

neighboring gardens, with fruits and berries from the groves and shubberies. The lawn is tasteful in croquet and tennis plats, shade and shubbery and tropical plants, with bowling and billiard rooms. Good saddle and carriage horses are supplied, and steam, sail and row boats on the adjacent lakes. The artist has perhaps better defined the character of the hotel than the penman, in his sketch on page 14.

But these worthy gentlemen in their ideal transfer of the best New York society en bloc to the climate of Florida, show a profounder sense of what is the vital informing spirit of that noble old Knickerbocker sentiment than in the mere catering to physical wants. They have founded a collegiate institute, under the presidency of Rev. E. P. Hooker, D. D., supported by a learned corps of Northern instructors. The telegraph, post and news offices are in the hotel, which we cordially commend to visitors.

But we turn from such studies to the natural and cultivated charms of the country, which it owes to no fortuitous cause. Nothing is more graceful and alluring to the worn out man of business, weary of stocks and bonds and anxious to see God's world without the stucco and plaster, than the lazy gathering and clarifying of our South Florida pools and water courses, and there is no prettier or more romantic group than those forming Howell's Creek and the Wekiva. The casual visitor who glances from the car window at the graceful building and rank groves of Winter Park, brightens as his eye rests on the broad avenue leading down into the cool, dark recesses of pleasure beyond. The changed foliage, the deeper vendure, its familiar massing, recall boyish holiday times by the waterside. Stale old magazine verses like these come to mind, about trout fishing:

> " Alas! that love which we remember,
> Blush ripe as all these wanton weeds,
> Should be a blossom of September,
> Born guiltless of the promise seeds.
> A dying thing, whose only duty
> Was clothing life in forms of beauty;
> For though I held you in my arms,
> As full of honey in your charms,
> As when the trefoil holds the clover;
> Your fingers tutored in a thimble,
> In playing trout were found so nimble,
> You caught the fish and cast the lover."

Indeed, yes,

> " Our lives have grown to other needs,
> Our boat lies rotting in the weeds,
> And we can neither raise nor row it."

But who of us that sees a mountain brook or shadowy loch but confesses to an atavism of the old fountain worship. Among the picturesque scenes of the vicinity, our artist has chosen that which represents the canal cut near Winter Park, between Osceola and Virginia. (See page 15.) A very little dredging would open a water transit by Howell's Creek to the St. Johns; but let us confess to Ruskinism, so far as to hope the work will be limited to flumes for picturesque water mills. That sweet old local self-supporting fashion of our fathers, with its mossy dripping wheel and dry straw-scented granary is vanishing in the serenities of old men's memories.

Among the familiar scenes of the season about Fort Reid, Jesup, then Lake Charm and on beautiful Conway is the orange. What is called the June orange is in blossom after the February apple is as large as a walnut in its green husk. A consequence is that the orange harvest, beginning in October, continues till the following February or March, and the writer has ripe fruit on the tree in May. This liberality in maturing and preserving its juices on the tree has been too little studied in harvesting. The fruit is hurried on the market in an imperfect fruition.

But no season or task is more pleasant. The fruit must be " stem cut," and the spectacle of crowds of gatherers hidden in foliage, bearing a haversack in front, is lively and engaging. From this it goes to the drying house

LARGEST ORANGE TREE IN FLORIDA, NEAR PLANT CITY.

and is " sweated " or suffered to dry on paling shelves exposed to a dry air.
Then it is selected by machinery ; strips from an inch and a half interval between, that widens its parallax to three inches, set at a gentle incline, drop each
apple at the space open to the width of its diameter into a sack. From these
they are taken and the separate sizes wrapped in tissue paper and packed in
light elastic boxes.   These boxes range from 120 to 200 apples to a crate.
But great care is taken first to separate all bruised, thorn pricked and de-
fective fruits.   Then after drying and sizing is separation into orders of bright
fancy, fancy russet, choice russet, down to the average orange that in flavor
equals the others ; but its coat is neither bright nor russet, but dull and
freckled.   Then they are carted to the station and shipped to such market as

the commission merchant chooses to make or report. The annual increment of shipment from this and the adjoining counties is enormous, and yet it forms scarcely an integer in the world's market. The glut is always local, the prices varying one or two dollars per box at points contiguous, as Boston, Philadelphia and New York.

In production of Southern staples, cotton ranges at 500 pounds per acre. Oranges, arranged in grove form, eight yards apart, will contain 72 trees to the acre. If we estimate a bearing grove at 500 apples, or three and a half boxes to the tree, 3½ multiplied by 72 is 252 boxes per acre, which at 80 pounds per box is 20,160 pounds per acre. That is, one acre of the fruit fills a freight car, which it takes 40 acres of the staple to fill.

The next station, by handsome grounds on the east and a lake on the west, is Wilcox, but we may now dispense with subdivisions, we are in Orlando. A mile or two more and the train draws up amidst a frenzy of negro hotel drummers, shouting the excellence of their entertainment, at the handsome depot.

ORLANDO.

The growth of Orlando is phenomenal. It stands unrivalled in Southern city growth. No great factory, no mine or oil well draws a factitious or dependent population. Its entire capital is the wealth of the surrounding groves and truck gardens, and its unrivalled climate. It has built no road; it has established no public fair; has never spent a farthing in printers' ink. It has founded no college nor other public institute to invite population, yet all these things have come to it. In fact, Orlando is the creation of the individual enterprise of her private citizens, entirely independent of the municipality. Seated at the parting of the waters, the young city has rested on her superb natural advantages. If she has built no public park she can point to her throne in the midst of sixteen fair lakes within her limits, and grand orange groves on her streets, and claim that Orlando is all park, the most beautiful park in the world.

Attention was called to it in a series of letters, from 1870 to 1877, to the Cincinnati *Commercial* and the Boston *Courier*, and it became a resort for invalids suffering with rheumatic, asthmatic and lung diseases. It used to be pitiful, pathetic, to see them sitting about in the open pine woods, that Orlando then was, enjoying the pungent breath of the amber scents and enjoying the rich southern sunshine. Mr. Summerlin built the court house at a time the cash for it was county scrip, and added the Summerlin House, pleasantly situated on Lake Eola. The South Florida Railroad opened travel. It is the keynote to Orlando's prosperity, for as the fruit growers prospered, their superfluous gains were invested in fine stores and warehouses. The visitor can hardly find a handsome store, hotel or bank that does not go back directly to the orange grove. Others contributed. A tourist and his family, spending his summer vacation, was pleased with the situation and bought an acre in town, beginning to build. Before the carpenters were out of the houses they were sold and the capital doubled. The fame of transactions, familiar and frequent as this, was a more active publication among visitors, speculators, settlers, than the press. It was sound because it rested on the abundant fruitfulness of its groves and gardens.

Perhaps Orlando itself was never just as thoroughly surprised as

33

at the success of its own impromptu fair in 1887. The proposal arose casually, without preparation, and after a little conference a committee undertook the matter. The South Florida Railroad promptly advanced to its aid, grading its fares at excursion rates that dispensed with entrance fees. The means was promptly furnished. But it was not until the rival southern counties, Polk, Hillsborough, Hernando, Sumter, Volusia, Manatee, Brevard, began to pour in their splendid display, and the hotels and private residences to overflow, that the committee realized what a tremen-

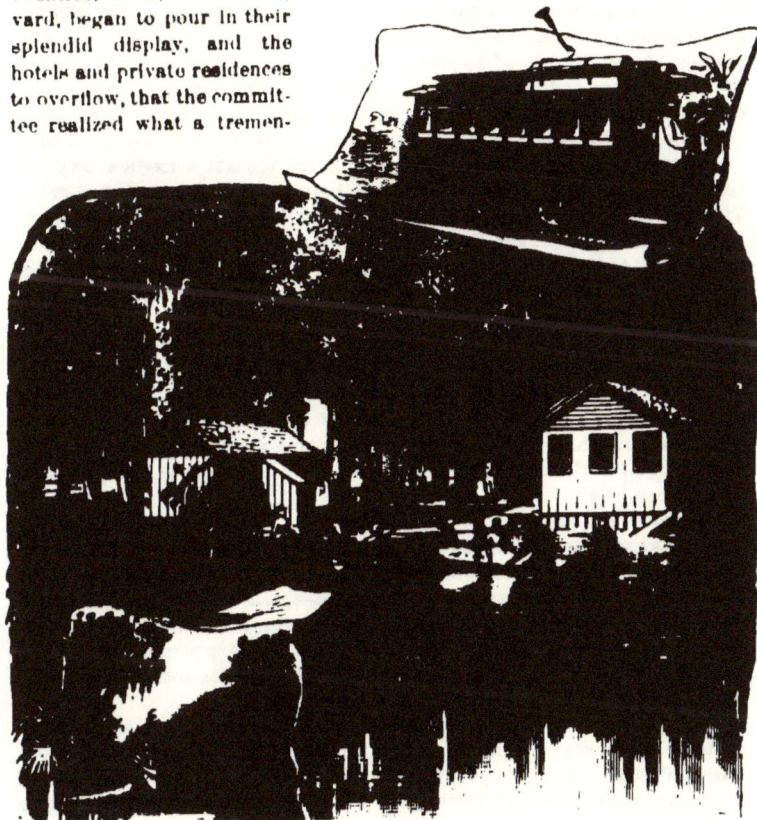

KISSINGEE SPRING, NEAR BARTOW.

dous bonanza it was. The exhibition, if faulty in that inadequate preparation, was brilliant as a show of what South Florida can do, upon a sudden inspiration. Our artist gives an inside view, to be luxuriously multiplied many times.

Orlando is built of the peel of the orange. Next to that unquestionably it owes its prosperity to the enterprise and liberality of the South Florida Railroad, which put a spinal column in the inchoate mass of throbbing vitality in Orange county, and bade it stiffen up, arise and go about its business.

The main street, a beautiful perspective, extends from Wilcox Station, or the Waterworks hill, above Lake Concord, south to where Hughey's grove makes an awkward deflection of its rectilineal beauty. The young city is lighted, and has waterworks, street cars, telephones, court house and county and city buildings, a handsome armory, opera house, handsome churches of elaborate interior finish of native woods and stained glass, a measured two miles. The original incorporation contemplated a circular area of a measured one mile radius from the court house. This was plotted in 500 feet blocks, but the private interest that has been the active architect of this city building has constantly interrupted a projection that the numberless lakes in the city limits rendered difficult. The names in the main block between Tampa or Railroad Avenue and Magnolia, amputated to Main by crosstrees, like a main mast, are, beginning north: Sweet, Concord, Amelia, Livingston, Robinson, Jefferson, Washington, Central, Pine, Church, South, Lucerne Avenue, a continuation of America, Ernestine, Irene and Anne, the last a diagonal cross to Lake Copeland. The business center is between Washington and Church. Two railroads, the Tavares and Orlando and the South Florida, join on Tampa Avenue. Orange, between Tampa and the crosstrees of Main and Magnolia, and parallel to them, is the street of banks and dry goods stores, and of the Arcade, a beautiful shipshape hotel, with graceful awnings and light, airy chambers for a hundred guests.

The Kedney Building, a handsome brick block of warerooms, deep, cool vestibule and hotel quarters above, on the same street, will probably open to as many. Besides these are the old Summerlin, a cool retreat on Lake Eola, with rooms for twenty-five guests, and the Lucerne, delightfully placed to front the acorn shaped Lake Lucerne, and having a charming view from its airy front, a favorite of the Southern guests, from Louisiana to Kentucky, and many others.

In order to appreciate the lovely site on which the city stands, the guests should ascend to the top of the Armory building on Court Street, and discover the picturesque surroundings of lake, orange grove and pinewoods. It is the seat of the county records and has a good conservative Mayor and Council, a daily press, the *Record*, two weeklies, the *Reporter* and *Sentinel*, and is admirably policed, ventilated and drained. There are many pleasant drives and picnic grounds in the vicinity; a street railway connects with Winter Park, and new avenues are opening up in every direction.

As the train draws out by lumber yards and planing mills, it skirts pretty cottages and lawns and suburban villas, the dark green of the orange dominating at every turn. We pass Maj. Foster's grove, the orchards of orange, lime, lemon, LeConte pear, closing like a sea at each side; pass Troy, sitting by the lake shore, down a spacious avenue, Lake Holden gleaming in view, and the summit reservoir of the county, Lake Conway, shows its upper basin under the vaulted pines; Gatlin Station to the site of old Fort Gatlin, named from Dr. Gatlin, a victim of Dade's massacre, Christmas Eve, 1835. The story is that in the second attack, "Lieut. Bassinger continued to fire the six-pounder until all the men who served the piece were shot. Capt. Gardener at length fell. Dr. Gatlin with two double-barreled guns continued to fire on the Indians until he fell late in the action and Lieut. Bassinger was wounded." The site of the fort is on a knoll between two beautiful lakes, and projecting into a third. Twenty years ago the cellar and some vestige of the brick bake

34

house and parade ground were traceable, but nature has again and again re-
sumed her domination over this once key to the Indian kingdom of Philip
and his gallant son Cooacoochee, the Wild Cat ; but the spot is still consecrated
and holy ground ; the remains of Hon. W. M. Randolph and wife, to whose
energy and forethought the opening up of settlements at this point and Fort
Reid is due, lie in its shadowy groves.

The banks make a sheer descent, free of marsh grass, to the lake about
it, and its commanding site gives a wide view of the broad basin of Conway,
winding like a broad river, by hammock, villa, grove and islands, eight or ten
miles south. This is a favorite location for fish fries, picnics ; and the Orange
Regatta use the beautiful stretch east to Bay Mizell as their coursing waters.

SCENE ON LAKE ARIANA, AUBURNDALE.

The region, and especially the west side, is a favorite resort. The peninsula
with a little orange grove on its shoulder at Mecharney, like an epaulette, is an
epitome, a typical picture of a hammock. The great live oaks, water oaks, wild
plums, are overgrown with wild yellow jasmine, forming natural arcades and
alleys, and beautiful wooded coves, swept by long hyacinthine grasses or
white with a snow of lilies on them. The railroad line, between lake shore
and orange grove, aligns the shore, and at Jessamine passes W. R. Anno's
handsome house and grounds, enclosed between the two large basins of Conway and Jessamine, having a natural fishpond on its southern orchard. The
plain little village church and school on a high, airy point, comes next, and
the village post office, quiet country inn, handsome warehouse, with farm
houses, fields of sugar cane, for which the area was once famous, and the remote peaks of the old castle, from which the village is named, scarcely visible
at the lake shore on the east. The west is a high plateau with a show of sugar
cane under the aisles of pine, and shallow pool and marsh. We are at the

farming lands, where one sees occasionally the old staples; not for the market, however, but for home use. A stretch of groves reach from the old castle, a half mile or more, lining the west shore of the lake, and a peninsula opposite its front shows a picturesque residence bedded in the trees. Far south is the handsome home and residence of the English gentry, adjoining the grove of Mr. Alexander, of Louisville, Ky. The fruitfulness, the suggestions of this little Western Galilee is full of suggestive verse, which we copy from an old *Atlantic Monthly*:

FLORIDA MIDNIGHT.

" The rain floats off; the crescent moon
  Holds in its cup a round of dusk,
  Like palm bud in the month of June,
  Half breaking from a vernal husk;
  Night blooming agave parts the sheaf,
  To catch the light distilled in showers,
  Till, overflowing cup and leaf,
  Its cluster breaks in midnight flowers.

" Like merchants breaking kids of nard,
  And jars of olives, desert born,
  Pine apples lift a prickly shard,
  And show the seeds of fragrant corn,
  While breathes a low, sweet undertone,
  Like brooks that grieve through beds of fern,
  As if, by curve and pebble stone,
  The moon had spilled her silver urn.

" Like Hebrew maids, the citrons hold
  Their pitchers to the vapor spring,
  And fill their hollow rinds of gold
  With midnight's musky offering.
  So once, I think, earth knew her Lord
  In lands like these of palm and vine,
  When midnight gave the sweet accord
  That turned the water into wine." .

The train slides down the divide between Boggy and Shingle creek, through a sparsely settled region, not yet fully redeemed from the cattle men and small holders, who do a stroke of business occasionally in having their stock run over by a train. The road pays for this jerked beef; and asks no questions, so all parties are satisfied. It is fine in yellow pine and naval stores, and there are large bodies of fine arable land. Example is seen at McKinnon, a way station, post office and saw mill, having young groves about it. Six miles beyond, under an arch and green tunnel of hamack growth, and Lake Tohopekaliga breaks in view, with its long, low green shore, its clustered islands, and the shining city of Kissimmee in the foreground.

Kissimmee City dates substantially from 1883. It had been settled before. Old Ivan Ericson, a Norwegian, whose exploration of the shell mounds is referred to by Brinton, located on it when it was a cow range. Mr. Robert Bass cleared and settled on the hammock in 1870, and Maj. Allen, Sr., a year or two later. In 1881-2 Capt. R. E. Rose, of the Okeechobee Drainage Company, brought his young family to the wild, and began boldly the construction of boats, dredges and revision and repair of works necessary to the gigantic undertaking. This courage and the novelty of the enterprise of draining an area half as large as the New England States attracted general attention. The South Florida Railroad had already struck out for this point, contemplating the Kissimmee river as a good water adjunct, corresponding to the St. Johns, to their line. Col. Aderhold erected a hotel, and curious visitors flocked in. Mr. W. A. Patrick bought a press, built and improved an addition to the town laid off by the railroad. But the union of the South Florida Railroad in the Plant Investment Company's construction from that point to Tampa of a railroad, diverted attention from the river route, and there appeared to be a lull. At that time Mr. Patrick's press was taken in charge and the *Bitter-Sweet* founded, the publisher joining in the energetic protest of Capt. R. E. Rose and others that Kissimmee City was the natural and necessary headquarters of the great drainage scheme.

It led, after some correspondence with Mr. Forbes, Mr. Disston and parties in interest, to the appointment of Mr. William Cannon to the land agency at Kissimmee City. No more striking or important service was done to the young city at a critical juncture than this appointment. The municipal incorpation was reformed, officered, the town platted, streets ditched and drained, and by January, 1885, it assumed the appearance of a charming little city destined to grow. The price of lands rose 600 per cent., a national bank was established, population reduplicated, and rose from an electoral vote of nine to some three hundred, and rows of handsome business houses were built in every part of the town. It is now one of the liveliest, most progressive young cities in South Florida, of some 2,000 population; the prospective county seat of the new county of Osceola, supported by a rich country in the thousands of acres of newly drained lands, especially adapted to sugar cane. The revival of that favorite staple promises to add a source of wealth to South Florida, rivalling the orange. Capt. R. E. Rose had, in the present year (1887), two hundred acres in cane and fifty or sixty in corn, on land he had crossed over in his steamboat two years before. A plant for centrifugal evaporator and refinery is in course of construction, and is perhaps completed by the time the reader follows these lines. The set of the year 1888 will be by Capt. Rose 700 acres, and his successful manipulation cannot fail to bring to Florida the sugar planters of Louisiana, thus freed of the dangerous floods of the Mississippi.

The Tropical Hotel, with accommodation for 125 guests, is one of the most beautiful of Southern hotels, most beautifully located. Fronting on the bright waters of Lake Tohopekaliga, in the midst of a graceful lawn among the pines, from its lofty observatory above, the whole ample panorama lies mapped in vivid color. Yachts, sail and row boats are furnished and there are hundreds of points accessible to the sportsman or pleasure parties. Ferries run to Southport, at the lower end of Lake Tohopekaliga, and connect with transportation to the English colony of Narcoossee, on East Tohopekaliga. A steam packet runs to Fort Bassinger, T. 36, R. xxx; Lat. 27 deg., 15 min., touching at Whitemore, Floridelphia, Shivers, Brahma Island, Stewartstown and Guy's Landing; and a new steamer is in construction to run to Floridelphia and Lake Tiger. No more interesting point for observation or pleasant excursions into a new, unpruned wilderness than Kissimmee City exists in

South Florida. A battle was fought here, or a skirmish with the Indians, in 1837-8. The dead were buried, it is said, in the tumulus on the South Florida Railroad just south of town.

The train skirts the lake shore among the green trails of the hill streams, finding their way by Reedy, Bonnet, Shingle and a thousand threads to the lake. How expressive a rivulet is, whether in straitened aqueducts, a mere porter of mankind, or in its natural physical and artistic sense; even the barren sand is sketched in the graceful ripple mark, or shaded in delicately fine shading like a line engraving. Yet its full expressiveness, its picturesque and physical beauty is only attained in the fine color lines of vegetation. The appositeness of the suggestion is shown most in the strange palm and oak hamacks that line our roads, pools, and soft meadows of spongy green, laid in delicate palette colors on the burnt umber of the pine background. Constantly in crossing the broad, oozy bottoms of Reedy, Shingle and Bonnet creeks we observe the humors of moist shading in the innumerable tones of green. The variety developed in one single hamack is wonderfully expressive, and is brightened by such picturesque sites as Campbell's Station.

Mr. Campbell is a pioneer settler, and was a Confederate soldier as stubborn and impregnable in battle, as provident and industrious as a planter. Bearing twelve wounds on his person, his hardihood, something in his bold, genial character, recalls Dandie Dinmont, of Charlie's Hope, in Scott's novel of Guy Mannering; nor is the otter hunt, and the prime Pepper and Mustard breed lacking.

Scenery of character so peculiar cannot fail of historic association. The grade across these quaking mosses must have been impracticable to all but the light footed Indian. It is associated with an incident of de Soto's march, the night ride of Gonsalvo de Silvestre. De Soto had found a bridge, a fallen log across the morass, and crossed with his advanced guard. He now said to the young cavalier: "To your lot has fallen the best horse in the army, and the more work you will have in consequence, for we have to assign you the most difficult tasks that occur. Return and tell Luis de Moscoro to follow us with the army and to dispatch you ahead with provisions for our supply." That bold night ride, after passing a "vast plain" west of Ichipuchisassa, near Plant City, ran parallel to the present railroad line. The Wahoo, or Holy Swamp, which de Soto attempted north of Ichipuchisassa, and failed, lies between Long. 82 deg., 15 min. and 81 deg., 45 min., and Lat. 28 deg., 10 min. and 28 deg. 30 min., forming not only the source of the Withlacoochee, but of Hawks, falling into the Ocklawaha, Horse, Davenport, Reedy into the Kissimmee, and Calos (Charley) Apopka and Peace Creek, falling into Charlotte Harbor. All of these, including the Beach Water branch of the Hillsborough, emptying into Tampa Bay, flow to every point of the compass from an exact center on the Sand Hills, Lat. 28 deg., 12 min., Long. 81 deg., 40 min., within a mile or two of old Fort Davenport. The army maps show the trails, and there was none other for de Soto, nor indeed for the railroad grade but that taken. Historians who traced the route ignored the itinerary, which carries the march north and east, or northeast from Ichipuchisassa, the old Foxtown settlements in Hillsborough. The twelfth chapter of Irving's narrative is an admirable local description of the diffi-

LAKE HOLLINGSWORTH, LAKELAND.

culties encountered by the engineers of the Plant Investment Company in building the road. The Sand Hills form the crest of South Florida 250 feet above the sea. The railroad grade ascends by the first steppe or terrace, ranging from 65 feet at Lake Tohopekaliga to 210 feet at Lakeland. A series of beautiful lakes and pools are formed on this and the succeeding terraces, acting as windows or ventilators, renewing the salt freshness of the Gulf wind. As we leave Campbell's by some meadows into a covert of cabbage palms lifting their tufted tops above the rank, sodden pools, we pass a saw mill and Lake Locke. Residences and farms appear and far stretches of vision across some lake. An energetic settler and English company have cut three and one-half miles of canal and are engaged in redeeming these meadows, which will be astonishingly fertile.

Davenport Creek is the high point 250 feet above the sea. We cross a swale by a round pool, and pass a line of fence and into a stretch of rolling lands, entering to Haines City, showing the neat, handsome improvements common to the line. We pass more hamacks and open woods, and the houses cluster more thickly at Bartow Junction. It is a high, breezy point with a charming highland lake, which our artist has caught, but no photo can show the miles of shining water, like a river in the hills, and the vegetation fresh with verdure as if newly washed.

We sweep down the open pine woods on the Bartow branch to try the new connection. The land is rolling, the great river-like lake still visible until we dip into spongy marsh meadows, and rushes lying in great breadths of green, like a rough sketch of the Carolina rice meadows we crossed en route for Savannah. The land rolls in smooth, round waves, and in each hollow is a broad, bright pool, like Arthur's shield, Lakes Cummings, Canon, Shipp, Howe, Eloise. In this way we dip by open pines, and by another lake, like the fragment of some favorite river the emigrant found it impossible to part with, and so brought it South with the rest of his penates. There is a handsome church; a land office like a cocked hat; a school house, and pretty, picturesque residences in paling fences. It is Winter Haven, and you recognize it with pleasure as the prospective site of the South Florida Presbyterian College. We leave the string of bead-like lakes, under a smoky light, only to see another with a wool of mossy foliage stooping from high banks to the water, and come into the flat woods. They look like forest fastnesses, so dark, gloomy, and untamed in their recesses; but the golden light flows in it and through it and over a lovely terrace crowned with a handsome station and depot, and a bright lake like a new fallen moon. It is pretty enough to provoke question, and our artist has preserved it.

There is a family likeness in these forest scenes to the landscape in Orange; but it has also its characteristics. The hard-wood trees which are found clustered in hamacks in Orange, and overgrown with parasitic growth, are more separated in Polk. It makes a variety in masses of foliage more like forests further North. The ground; we do not mean the soil, but the tone of reflection that strikes the eye, is darker, blacker. The live oaks are noble, massive trees, and isolation has preserved their natural forms and arrangement of branches. We pass mottes of them; by rural homes in cane and groves surrounding them. Familiar country roads cross, but carefully

40

avoid any such intimacy as strolling along side by side. In this way, we enter a swale or bay, and out of its moist, spongy greenness, over a dry skinned woodland, to a pretty depot ; a rather humble country inn, and you are at Bartow. No, it is on the outskirts of Bartow, whose peaks and gables show a half mile south. But a 'bus attends and the traveler is soon made comfortable at the Charleston.

Bartow is older than Orlando, and until the development of orange culture was the center of a thriving population of farmers and cattle men. The herds feeding on the flat, grassy meadows of Peace Creek or the numberless crab grass swales that interlie the numberless lakes, were herded in season at Bartow and driven to Tampa or Charlotte Harbor, for shipment to Cuba. In the palmy days of the cattle kings of Orange, Polk, Hillsborough, Manatee and Dade, a failure in delivering Florida stock, which arose sometimes from jealously of the authorities in Cuba, led to an invasion of the Texas carvayals by the Mexican ranchers ; banditti gathered in Texas the adequate demand. But those days are among the ashes of burnt out fevers, and Bartow is now the promising center of orange culture in Polk. The town site is unique and beautiful. A broad, flat hump, two miles by one, inclines gently

WITHLACOOCHEE RIVER.

but perceptibly to a green border of cedar, live oak and hamack growths. This smooth campus is regularly laid off in broad avenues handsomely built up in stores and warehouses, surrounding the court house. The view

BRIDGE OVER WITHLACOOCHEE RIVER.

WITHLACOOCHEE RIVER, AT PEMBERTON FERRY.

south and west includes picturesque, vine-clad cottages in the soft greys of weathered wood, blending with tones and undertones of live oak and orange ; or the dark, secluded coverts of the town wall of green hamack. Nothing adds so much to the intrinsic beauty of the place as the stately live oaks and water oaks that grace its broad streets and avenues. A town hall or opera house is among the public buildings, and the religion is housed and officered

41

in the parsonages and churches of Rev. Mr. Hair, of the Presbyterian Church South ; Rev. Mr. Dye, Baptist ; Rev. Mr. Nixon, Methodist ; Rev. Mr. Fitzhugh, Episcopal.

A handsome school building, founded on the liberal donation of Mr. J. L. Summerin, of Orange, builder of the Court House and hotel in Orlando, is recently completed. The press is represented by the *Advance-Courier* and the Bartow *Informant*, energetic and progressive representatives of the thriving district. Among the opportunities to the excursionist is a trip down the Florida Southern to Forts Meade, Ogden and the new port of Punta Gorda, on Charlotte Harbor; among the velvety Mangrove Islands; above Fort Myers ; the bay and the intervening valley of Peace Creek, abounding in game, from the cougar to the pink curlew, and ducks thick as mosquitoes.

A pleasant picnic excursion is one to the famous Kissingen Spring, near Bartow. This beautiful fountain, a hundred feet across, is on an open hammock of live oaks and water-loving trees, the dark bluish water forced up to make an inverted dish surface, the water slipping smoothly from its dish like a watch crystal.

Returning to Bartow Junction the road passes through a lovely wild scenery of lakes, made attractive by charming villa sites, by park-like open pines, as free of undergrowth as a trimmed lawn, or by green coverts of the deer, and where the slender cougar lies in wait for the doe, at the watering places. No one knows better than the hunter, unless it is the " painter " itself, that animals are as much or more the slaves of habit than men. If a buck has followed a certain course, three to one he will be over it again; points to remember in these hunting grounds. In the cluster, but on the broad hump among them, is pretty Auburndale, laid out with curved and straight avenues, like the spokes and felloes, on concentric rays, so as to utilize the building sites. It shows the characteristic thrift and energy of these Southern towns, a spirit that would make a desert prosperous, and in these fertile, hospitable hills cannot fail to prosper. The success of Orange county shows that Polk in these environs can do as well.

We pass on to Fitzhugh, a charming site among the woodland lakes, with the new grove under picket and paling, and the dreamy little chateaux—no other word describes the quaint, pretty architecture we sometimes see, where native fancy suits the landscape.

Lakeland unites to its natural advantages and present opportunities as the junction of the main line and Pemberton branch of the South Florida Railroad, the prospective hope of drawing to it the associate lines of the West Coast. The town is more city-like than any point north of it. It is laid off about a main plaza forming a square of some ten acres, with the railway extending along one thoroughfare. The business blocks fill the public square, the avenues extending out and beyond being occupied with residences and groves. There are a number of these, and the place has such an air of established dignity, belonging to mature development, it is hard to believe the babe born the day it was incorporated is yet in long clothes ; or that four years ago there were more wild cats and panthers than men and women in the city. But it represents a number of intelligent capitalists and business men, who have identified themselves with it, and it has become the market town

42

and shipping point of the greater part of Polk county. The truck garden interest makes its handling an important and growing interest. It sustains a handsome weekly paper, a large school, and prosperous Christian community.

Lakeland is undoubtedly on the "high plain" described in the Incas narrative, from which de Soto "sent out runners ahead to explore the route. The latter returned the next day, declaring that they could not proceed further, on account of the many bogs made by the streams which ran out of the great morass and inundated the country." Their exploration must have been on the north, and the path found by de Soto from a guide must have been the old

PICNIC GROUNDS, TAMPA

trail to Fort Mellon, because de Soto was encumbered, having "besides armor, military stores, camp equipage, with three hundred swine. . . These animals were placed in charge of a company of horse to keep them in line of march and guard them

DE SOTO SPRING.

in traversing swamps and rivers." To cross Wahoo Swamp north of Lakeland with such an impediment was plainly impracticable.

But the Pemberton's Ferry Branch, after some feats of engineering, takes that course. Lakeland is across the sand hills, about three miles from Ichipuchiassa. Our course is through a wild, watery wilderness, crossing the Hillsborough, or turning it north of Teddersville. If, however, we err in this, we are on the direct trail of de Soto, and of the more memorable march of Dade's command, Christmas Eve, fifty-two years ago. The treacherous Indians were to rendezvous in the great Wahoo Swamp; and that dark green line, now making salient near the road, and now a re-entering curve, is the river dividing us from it. We pass a number of farms in cultivation. The

43

land seems unusually fertile; good corn land. It is a marl and differs altogether from the loamy lands in Polk and Orange. It is undoubtedly a better grain country; the meadows are in grass and the stations are admirably chosen for beauty, healthfulness, fertility. They are all either on a gentle slope or a green meadow, with white headstones to mark the survey, making them look dreadfully like pretty cemeteries. They are natural truck farms and the visitor is not surprised to see crates of green vegetables at Kathleen and Feddersville. Richland lies on a gentle slope, a beautiful green lawn, with handsome improvements suggesting the appropriateness of the name. A young orange grove lies out from Dade City, and there are fences and farmed fields, and deep green hamacks follow, with beautiful live oaks standing on moist, spongy pastures. The wild cattle toss their horns and go scurrying off, but so lightly on the springy turf they seem to fly. By Owensboro, Macon, Oriole, laid out in regular streets and squares, and to the long, broad awning, red-roofed station and depot at Pemberton's Ferry. It was here Maj. Dade's command, " on the 27th reached the Withlacoochee and camped." They had marched six miles in open order. Three weeks later Captain Hitchcock found the dead as they lay firing from the breastworks—thirty dead bodies. Major Dade and Captain Frazer a little farther with the advance guard. The command was literally wiped out. It was the tragedy of Custer's command anticipated. It was from here they set out that high Christmas week. But at this very point, a month later, Gen. Gaines with six companies was besieged for a week, till rations were reduced to one pint of corn per day, and meat rations of horse beef and dog pork. Let us turn from those fierce old tales.

Mr. Pemberton established himself at the ferry in 1875 and began his clearing. In 1877-8 he got a post office by becoming security, and diverted the Tampa mail by this route. His enterprise induced others, and the surrounding area is well set in some ten thousand orange trees. The Government is engaged in clearing out and rendering the Withlacoochee navigable to this point, which will contribute greatly to the lumber interest, by bringing the grand groves of cedar, cypress, Florida mahogany, which line it, accessible. Fruit gardening is also a lively interest centering at this point, and the fishing and hunting are undoubtedly excellent. The present town is made up of some half dozen residences, two stores, the post office, depot and a large hotel for the entertainment of forty or fifty guests. There are five tracks laid at the junction, and a railroad bridge spans the river below the sawmill and ferry, and the scenery is one of the wildest, most romantic on the whole route. It is at the junction of the Florida Southern and South Florida roads.

The passage from Lakeland to Plant City crosses a spur of the sand hills and passes from the loam on to the marl lands of the coast. The town is one of surprising beauty, newness and activity. It competes with Lakeland in the intersection of the Florida Railway and Navigation line to Charlotte Harbor, and the South Florida, and central to the old Foxtown settlement of an older generation and the still older truck gardens and Spanish Mission at Ichipuohisassa, founds its present prosperity on the past. One of the evidences of this is a population of two thousand inhabitants. But its relation to the older colony and development is seen in an orange tree some six miles north,

44

which measures six feet seven inches in girth, four feet from the ground, and bore a crop the past season of *twelve thousand oranges*, of which eight thousand were sold in the Northern market and four thousand disposed of on the ground. Our artist has preserved the king of the grove.

This monster is said to be forty years old, and yet in the infancy of its development. In a hundred years it will be an orange grove in itself.

The ground slopes gradually by the suburban settlements of Seffner, Mango and Orienta, and we are at Tampa.

Tampa is probably older than St. Augustine. In the same year that Melendez founded the latter, his deputy, de Reinoro, was in charge at Tampa. We have the report of Melendez sending one hundred laborers to this point—including fifteen women—to teach the squaws to spin. Padre Rogel was in charge and in the following year Melendez made a truce between the Tozo

PARADE GROUND, OLD FORT BROOK, TAMPA

and Tampa tribes at Tocobayo. The peaceful, uninterrupted course of this colony would leave no record. In the study of Spanish colonization we must bear in mind that the base was at Havana. A fort was erected here on the beautiful reservation shown in the engraving. In 1835, and it was in the bay the interview between Cooacoochee and Gen. Worth occurred.

The bay is famous for its fish, the red snapper, grouper, sheepshead, red fish, black fish, pompano, Spanish mackerel, rock fish, mullet and a list of others noted for eccentric form or beauty. The oyster fisheries are choice, the game fine, though not large. The sponge fishery is an interest pursued by one or two, an individual enterprise, there being a prejudice against dredging schooners. The bouquet, silk, wire and finger sponge, are all taken along the sounds. The floor of the submarine world is gardened with rose coral, gorgonias, madrepore, flowery echinoderms; silver-like shells of

45

uvanilla, fusiform scalaria, trumpet shells, conchs, courie, olive, scollops and other bright or mottled shells.

Among the local industries is cigar and cigarette making, employing a large number of skilled workmen, an interest of large and growing importance to Florida, where the culture, cure and manufacture of the weed is in a manner native to the soil. Our artist presents a view of the interior of the factory.

Three large, handsome hotels offer their hospitality to the traveler. The Plant House, with accommodations for one hundred guests; the St. James, of equal capacity, and the Palmetto, of like roomy hospitality.

The great influx of travel at this important point, its central location as a distributing point to the coast, and the higher interest arising from the establishment of the Plant Investment line of steamers to Havana, insure the traveler of that hospitable care of the cuisine and comfort these hotels sup-

INTERIOR VIEW OF CIGAR FACTORY, YBOR CITY.

ply. The fresh salt air, a fish and oyster diet from the marine gardens of the beautiful bay, invite rest and recuperation; at the same time certain delightful excursions are offered.

The Sound steamer "Margaret" makes regular excursions for points on Tampa Bay, Manatee river and Egmont Key, points of romantic and curious interest to any one seeking health, relaxation or the wonderful development of South Florida. But the luxury of travel in Pullman Buffet sleepers on the West India fast mail requires one more additional luxury to complete it. As we have contrasted modern railway travel with the old fashioned stage coach and family carriage, it would be interesting to sketch our grandame's journey on the Royal Mail Packet "Eurydice," and her contemptuous comparison of the name of the muse with the dirt, discomfort and rudeness she was subjected to half a century ago.

The Plant Steamship Line, starting from this point, and carrying the West India Fast Mail, between Tampa, Key West and Havana, is composed of the steamships "Mascotte" and "Olivette," built by Crump & Co., of Philadelphia, and models of their class. Their hulls are of iron, laid in the most approved lines. Engines of the triple expansion type, especially adapted to the economy of power. The furniture is all of hard wood, highly finished, with chairs and sofas upholstered in leather. All the interior finishings are elaborate in hard wood panelling.

The illumination of these ships is by the Edison Incandescent light, with extra burners in case of accident. Electric bells in the staterooms communicate with the stewards and other proper quarters. Nothing has been left undone that would contribute to the ease and comfort of the traveler. They are the finest and most speedy ships of their class afloat, and there is no more enjoyable trip to the tourist than a visit to Key West and Havana via this line.

The entrance to the port of Havana is narrow but the harbor is deep, without any bar, and one of the finest in the world. The city lies along the entrance to and on the west side of the bay. The Moro and Punta castles guard the entrance; the city itself is fortified and the citadel is of great strength. These can only be visited by permits, but they are not refused, and the Spanish officers are gentlemen of great and chivalrous courtesy. Pleasant excursions by rail can be made to various parts of the island, the hotels furnishing all proper information.

TALLAHASSEE CHIEF OF SEMINOLES, AND TWO BOYS.

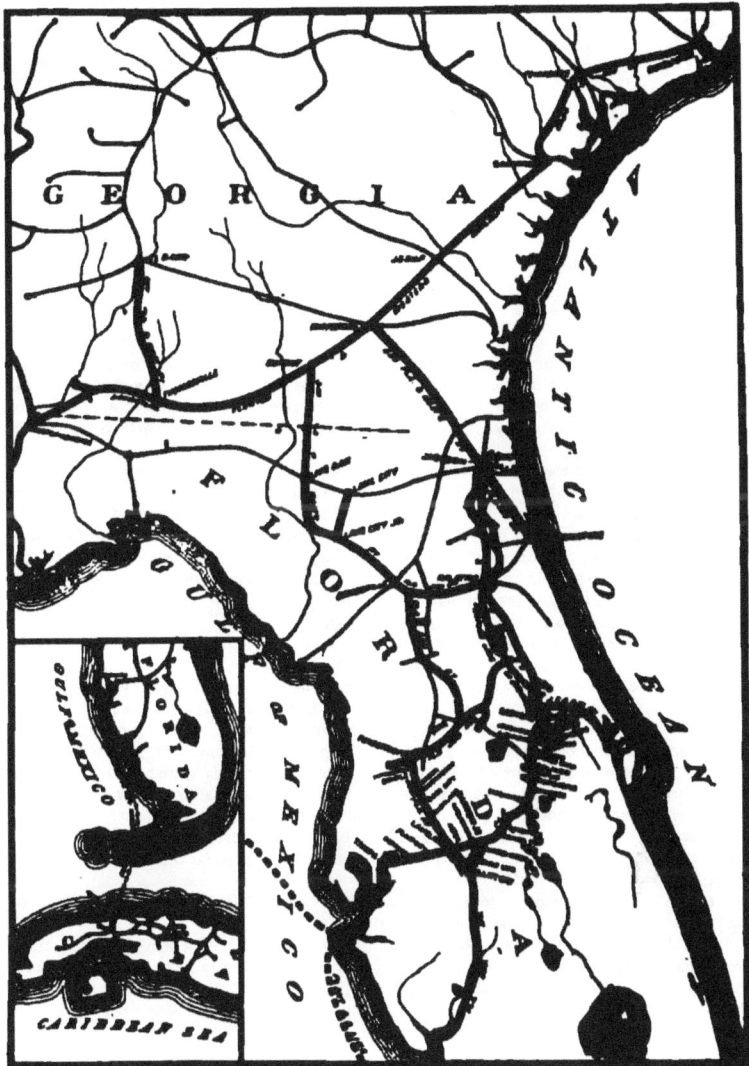

—MAP OF—
THE SOUTH FLORIDA RAILROAD
AND ITS CONNECTIONS.

THE SOUTH FLORIDA RAILROAD CO.

LAND DEPARTMENT.

The lands offered for sale by the Land Department of the South Florida Railroad, are varied in character, and suitable for every variety of tropical fruits and farming.

They embrace the richest pasture lands in the great grazing districts of Florida, and are offered in large or small tracts to suit purchasers, at prices within the reach of all.

The descriptive notes of the Peninsula, as given by counties, will give you but a faint idea of the wonderful resources of these lands. In the past two years, considerable attention has been paid to the growing of other fruits, not heretofore found among the list. Peaches, equal to any grown in the North, at the time of this writing, (May 6th), are putting on that delicate color and bloom which will soon cause to appear on the "Bill of Fare," "Peaches and Cream." Large orchards have been and are being planted. The time of ripening for the early varieties is from May 1st to May 15th; shipments will be made this year as early as May 10th.

In pears, the Le Conte and Kieffer varieties have been found by trial, to be excellent bearers—fruit of good quality, and to ripen about July 1st.

The Kelsey plum, rivaling in size, color and taste, the most famed varieties of California, is being cultivated largely and will prove a source of wealth to the grower.

With these mainstays, strawberries from January to June, and all other fruits in their season, it will be but a short time until Florida will be known far and wide as the "*banner fruit country of the world.*" In the quality of citrus fruits grown, Florida stands alone and unrivaled. It is unnecessary to enter into a discussion of their merits, for wherever known, Florida oranges are pronounced by all to be unequaled.

The growing of vegetables has become one of the prominent industries of the State. With the same application and care used by market gardeners in the North, the most bountiful yield may be had.

Does it pay? The answer to this question may be found in the market columns of any of the great dailies of the prominent cities.

Think of it, ye denizens of the North! During the long, cold winter there, while you are sitting around your furnaces and base-burners trying to keep warm, and wondering how many degrees it will go below zero "this time," the market gardeners of Florida are busy growing and shipping their fruits and vegetables, reaping a rich reward.

DESCRIPTIVE NOTES BY COUNTIES.

ORANGE COUNTY.

Orange County has for its northern and eastern boundary the St. Johns river, which gives it 100 miles of water transportation, and connects it with the Atlantic Ocean at Jacksonville. The western boundary passes through the great Lake Apopka. On the south it is bounded by the counties of Brevard and Polk. In point of elevation it ranges from 10 to 200 feet above the waters of the St. Johns river, rising by terraces to the center of the county. Owing to the advantages of its undulating surface and the consequent excellent natural drainage, its deep, clear water lakes, and peculiarly fertile soil, its salubrious climate and excellent water connections with the north, the tide of immigration, as early as the year 1870, commenced to flow in, and with a population in that year of only 2,195 as a nucleus it increased to 6,618 by 1880. At that time the South Florida Railroad was completed through the county, and contributed largely to the development of this beautiful section, as is shown by an increase of population from 1880 to 1885 of 8,813, the present population being 20,000. This road has brought in intelligent agriculturists, merchants, and citizens of every description; and the county now teems with industries which compare favorably with any section in the world.

In the fertile soil of this county almost every variety of *grain* can be raised, and especially is it adapted to the culture of oranges, lemons, limes, pineapples, and all semi-tropical fruits, too numerous to mention.

In this beautiful section, 83,639 acres of land are now offered for sale, from $1.25 to $10 per acre, such as lake fronts, lake views, on elevated ground for villa sites among the high table lands and hill region, tracts from 100 to 200 feet above sea level almost exempt from frosts, even when frosts are experienced in lower lands one hundred miles further south. Tender, tropical fruits can be grown *all winter* on these elevated plateaus. Also large bodies of low pine lands well timbered, flat lands, prairie and marsh lands, the latter being susceptible to drainage and are *very rich*, and upon which can be raised as fine sugar-cane as can be found in the world. Also large bodies of grazing land, producing luxuriant crops of valuable natural grasses.

We invite particular attention to our low pine lands with slight elevation, dry enough for oranges and farm and garden products. These are the most productive lands in South Florida, and oranges grown on them have no "off years," but *bear full every year.*

BREVARD COUNTY.

One of the largest in the State, and lying south and east of Orange, extending from Kissimmee river on the west to the Atlantic coast, and from the southern border of Volusia on the north to Dade county on the south. On the eastern side of this county lies the famous Indian river country. The elevation of this county varies from 10 to 100 feet above sea level, with general slope east and west, shedding its water through the St. Johns, Indian, St. Lucie and tributaries into the Atlantic, and Kissimmee river and Lake Okeechobee and Caloosahatchee river into the Gulf of Mexico. Climate about the same as Orange county. Surface flat, low, and much of it wet, the larger portion of the county being low prairie.

The population in 1880 was 1,478; in 1885, 2,376; increase in five years, 898. Principal industries, raising fruit, vegetables and cattle. In this county, 105,700 acres are controlled by the Land Department of the South Florida Railroad Company. They lie in the western portion, and are mostly rich prairie lands, well set in native grasses, affording fine ranges for large herds of cattle, and sufficiently high for drainage into the Kissimmee river, and are within the territory for which the Disston Drainage Company have contracted with the State of Florida to drain and make fit for cultivation.

SUMTER COUNTY

is situated in the interior portion of the peninsula, on the western slope of the "backbone" of the hill region, and abounds in beautiful lakes and high hills; is being rapidly settled, its population increasing from 4,486 in 1880 to 9,427 in 1885. Its climate, lands and products are similar to those of Orange county. This department now offers at prices from $1.25 to $5 per acre, 6,088 acres of land, most of which lie along the line between Orange and Sumter, among the hills and lakes of the "backbone" ridge, some having lake fronts; and others among the headwaters of the Palatlakaha, comprising beautiful ridges of rich land and dense hammocks and swamps.

POLK COUNTY.

The *midland* county of the peninsula, embracing an area of upwards of 2,000 square miles, covering the most inviting portion of the "backbone" hills and the celebrated lake region. It is celebrated for its *high hills* and deep, clear water lakes, the highest point on the South Florida Railroad being in this county near Lakeland.. These "high hills" among the deep lakes, are almost exempt from killing frosts, and for the production of tender tropical fruits and early vegetables they are especially adapted. The general surface of this county is undulating, and being the water-shed of the peninsula, large creeks and rivers running north, east, south and west have their sources among its hills and lakes. Some of the most productive agricultural lands are to be found along the valleys of these streams, and many of the higher undulating lands are of rich chocolate-colored loam underlaid with clay, and the early settlers sustained themselves by the products of their farms. Isolated as was this county until the construction of the South Florida Railroad in 1884, its population being only 3,181 in 1880, with very little increase until the completion of this road, yet in 1885 the population was found to be 6,623, an increase of 3,442. From a dull and lonely wilderness, this railroad has converted it into a most prosperous and thriving county. Bartow, the county seat, having quadrupled its population, replaced the old weather-beaten buildings of the past with neat and beautiful structures proportioned to the present state of thrift and enterprise; and quite in keeping with the balance, a commodious and handsome court house has been erected; two comfortable churches have been built, and a handsome school building is under construction. Fort Meade also seems to be struck by the magic wand of Progress, and is extending her borders on all sides. Lakeland, Auburndale, and Winter Haven, new-born heirs of railroad progression, will be more fully treated in the proper place. This department has now on the market in this county 105,569 acres of lands, which are being rapidly sold at prices ranging from $1.25 per acre for pasture lands up to $2.50, $5 and $10 an acre for ordinary farming and fruit lands, and $12 to $15 an acre for lake fronts near railroad stations and towns. These lands are especially desirable, as other railroads are now under construction through this country running at right angles to the South Florida Railroad.

HILLSBOROUGH COUNTY

is bounded on the east by Polk, on the west by the Gulf of Mexico, Hernando county on the north, and Manatee on the south. Its average elevation on the east is 150 feet above the sea, and slopes gradually west to the Gulf, into which it sheds its waters. It is eminently semi-tropical; Tampa, the county seat, being sixty miles further south than Sanford, in Orange county. The earliest settlement on the western coast of Florida was made in this county at Tampa, and at this place is the best harbor south of Pensacola. The lands in this county are very fertile and mostly well drained. Many of the desirable tracts were settled by thrifty farmers coincident with the settlement of Tampa, and for the past forty years have been self-sustaining, raising abundant crops of corn, sugar cane, rice, peas, potatoes, and all garden crops, besides all semi-tropical fruits. The site of each of the old homesteads is marked by a cluster of large, productive orange trees, lemons, grape-fruit and guavas. The Gulf Coast abounds in fish and oysters, and this last is becoming a great source of industry. In almost every river and tidewater creek oysters can be successfully planted. In 1884 the South Florida Railroad was completed through this county, running about midway between the fertile valleys of the Alafia and Hillsborough rivers, between which is a flattened ridge beginning at Lakeland in Polk county and extending to Tampa. This ridge slopes from near Lakeland (200 feet above sea level) gradually to tide-water, dropping off suddenly a few miles northward into Itchepuckesassa and Hillsborough rivers, and southward into the Alafia river, which facts put it within the reach of all land owners to thoroughly and easily drain their lands when necessary. In this county 41,818 acres of land are offered for sale, ranging in price from $1.25 to $25 per acre, according to location and quality of soil; convenience to depots and towns being an important item in fixing values.

HERNANDO COUNTY

bounded on the north by Marion, south by Hillsborough, west by the Gulf of Mexico and east by Sumter county. This county has as large a proportion of high, rich hammock and pine lands adapted to the cultivation of all plantation crops as well as semi-tropical fruits, as any other county in South Florida. Being without railroad communication until September, 1885, and having only its desirable location, high and fertile hills and valleys to induce immigration, it still attained an increase of population from 4,248 in 1880 to 7,173 in 1885. Now, with two railroads penetrating its borders, it is keeping pace with the neighboring counties in rapid development. In general features and climate it resembles adjoining counties of Hillsborough and Sumter. This department controls 9,133 acres of land in the county, besides the beautiful railroad town sites of Richland, Dade City, and Owensboro.

MANATEE COUNTY.

An empire in extent, being bounded on the north by Hillsborough and Polk counties, on the east by Brevard, south by Monroe and west by the Mexican Gulf. Area in round numbers, 5,220 square miles. The general surface is level, the highest lands lying near the northern boundary of the county and on the extension of the "backbone" ridge down to the west of Istokpoga lake and west of Peace Creek as far as Township 35 South. Soil varies from low, rich, black swamp, marsh, prairie, hammocks, low pine dry table, high chocolate pine and oak, scrub, and sand hills. Drainage through the Manatee, Myakka, Peace and Caloosahatchee rivers, Chilocoohatchee, Charlie Apopka, Bow Legs, Prairie, Fish Eating, Arbuckle and Istapoga Creeks; together with various tributaries. Though appearing level, low and wet to the unobserving traveler, this county is pierced in every direction by deep gulches, made by the water rapidly collecting from the surrounding country in the depressions, which sweeping toward their natural outlets, form the various streams already mentioned. Thus we see that this, one of the most fertile counties in South Florida, is susceptible of thorough drainage at the smallest expense, as nature ever lends a helping hand. Immense areas of land are being reclaimed in this county by the Okeechobee Drainage Company, through a system of canals now in course of construction. The soil and climate, to a greater extent than in any of the counties above referred to, are especially adapted to the culture of grasses and vegetables, and in a few years it is destined to become the garden and pasture of the State. This fertile section has been recently opened up by the Florida Southern Railroad, which penetrates its northern boundary and terminates at Charlotte Harbor. The tide of immigration has already commenced to flow in that direction. Rivers are being made navigable; thousands of dollars are being yearly expended; new life and enterprise is seen and felt on every side, and now is the accepted time to seize the splendid opportunity offered by the Land Department of this company, which controls 715,150 acres of land. Of this amount about three-fourths is grazing lands, affording the finest natural pasturage in Florida.

Besides the above-described lands this company has recently acquired about 250,000 acres lying in the counties Nassau, Duval, Columbia, Suwannee, Lafayette, Alachua, Marion, Hernando, Manatee, Polk and Monroe. The lands located in the northern counties have generally fine growths of pine timber, affording great inducements to saw-mill men. Large tracts in a solid body in Monroe and Manatee counties afford cattle ranges without limit, and special inducements are offered to cattle men who will purchase large bodies of land.

For further information, Folders, Maps, Prices, etc., address

GENERAL LAND AGENT SOUTH FLORIDA RAILROAD,
SANFORD, FLA.

THE ALTAMONTE HOTEL,

ALTAMONTE SPRINGS, ORANGE CO., FLA.

The prime feature of Altamonte as a resort, is its quietude. It is not a place widely advertised for the purpose of attracting the transient tourist, although, indeed, its picturesque scenes are such as abundantly to interest the seeker after the beautiful. But it is chiefly the resort of a large number of well-to-do Eastern and Northern men of business, who come for the perfect repose and quiet they get here. In this respect, there can be found no finer place than Altamonte; and among the hotel homes of the Orange State, there certainly is none more delightfully situated or more comfortable in its appointments than

THE ALTAMONTE HOTEL,

which begins its sixth season in the winter of 1887-8. The hotel is situated on a high plateau, some ninety feet above the St. Johns river, in an extensive grove of pines near the banks of two beautiful clear-water lakes, affording abundant opportunities for gunning, fishing, and boating, and commanding an outlook over miles of picturesque scenery. On the lake in front of the hotel has been placed a good steam-launch. In every direction are enjoyable walks and drives over some of the finest roads in the State, and through the ever-green woods and fragrant orange groves. Around the Altamonte Hotel are grouped a half-dozen or more fine cottages, occupied chiefly by their owners. The hotel rooms are furnished with gas and electric bells, and many of them with open fire-places. The house accommodates one hundred guests; and its manager, Mr. Frank A. Cofran, manager of the Twin Mountain House in the White Mountains, will make every possible provision for the comfort and enjoyment of the patrons. The *cuisine* is equal in every respect to that of the finest hotels in the country. Upon the table will be found the choicest cuts of beef and mutton that the New York and Boston markets afford, the delicious fish and oysters of Tampa Bay, fresh vegetables grown in the large garden attached to the hotel, eggs and poultry from neighboring farms, fresh milk and cream, oranges, lemons, strawberries, bananas, pineapples, and other fruits from surrounding orchards, and last, but not least, *the purest spring water* that anywhere flows from the ground. Horse cars run from the hotel to the railway station, half a mile distant. Connected with the hotel are a billiard and pool room, bowling alley, barber shop, livery stable, and steam laundry. From Sanford to Altamonte, there are three trains a day.

In short, it is believed that nothing has been neglected which might give comfort and restful enjoyment, an important consideration for guests.

"Orange County is to-day attracting more attention, and increasing faster in population, than any other county in the State."

ALTAMONTE SPRINGS

is situated on the South Florida Railroad, twelve miles south of Sanford, on the Fast Mail route to Tampa and Cuba. "The Altamonte" will open January 1st, 1888, and remain open till May 1st.

Terms, $4 per day, or $17.50 to $25 per week.

FRANK A. COFRAN, Proprietor.

Of THE TWIN MOUNTAIN HOUSE, White Mountains, N. H.

JACKSONVILLE, TAMPA & KEY WEST
RAILWAY.

WEST INDIA FAST MAIL ROUTE.

TRUNK LINE FROM JACKSONVILLE TO ALL POINTS IN SOUTH FLORIDA,

forming in connection with the South Florida Railroad, from Sanford, and its own branches and connections, absolutely the Best and Quickest Route to the following places :

ST. AUGUSTINE, PALATKA, DeLAND, TITUSVILLE, ROCKLEDGE AND ENTIRE INDIAN RIVER COUNTRY, SANFORD, TAVARES, ORLANDO, KISSIMMEE, BARTOW AND TAMPA.

SOLID TRAINS RUN FROM JACKSONVILLE TO TAMPA IN 8 HOURS carrying the Cuban Mails and Pullman Buffet Sleeping Cars, and connecting at Tampa with the magnificent Steamships " Olivette" and " Mascotte" for Key West and Havana three times a week.

ST. AUGUSTINE DIVISION—J. ST. A. & H. R. RY.

Air Line and only rail route from Jacksonville to St. Augustine. Four daily trains. Time, one hour and a half between the two cities.

Travelers from North and West arrive in Jacksonville Union Station (Savannah, Florida ank Western Railway) at which all main line trains of the Jacksonville, Tampa and Key West Railway arrive and depart, thus avoiding all vexatious transfers.

Transfer ferry boat to St. Augustine meets all trains at same station.

This road is built in the most substantial manner, and its passenger equipment is unsurpassed.

SEE THAT YOUR TICKETS READ VIA J.T.& K.W.RY.

For folders, maps of lands, of which this company owns over 2,000,000 acres, and all other information, call on or address any of the undersigned.

G. W. BENTLEY, Gen. Man.   M. R. MORAN, Gen. Supt.

ALFRED B. MASON, Land Commis'r.   L. C. DEMING, Gen. Ticket Agt.,

JACKSONVILLE, FLA.

"THE SEMINOLE," WINTER PARK, FLORIDA.

—Accommodations for 400 Guests.—

This elegant new hotel will open for guests *January 1st, 1886*.
Furnished in the most thorough manner, equipped with every modern convenience, the proprietors will spare no expense in their endeavor to make "THE SEMINOLE" first-class in every way, and *THE Resort for Florida Tourists*.

Located upon high land, covered with pines and orange groves; surrounded by beautiful lakes; with its College, Churches and Cottages its pure water and perfect drainage, Winter Park, for a winter home has no rival.
The fast mail with Pullman Buffet Cars through from New York to Winter Park without change in 44 hours.

FORBES & PAIGE, PROPRIETORS.

FISH, FOWL AND FUN

— IN —

FLORIDA, U. S. A.

DE BARY AND PEOPLE'S LINE STEAMERS

on St. Johns River.

DAILY SERVICE BETWEEN

JACKSONVILLE, TOCOI, PALATKA, ROLLESTON, WELAKA, ASTOR, DeLAND LANDING, BLUE SPRINGS, SANFORD AND ENTERPRISE,

and all landings on St. Johns river. Iron and steel hulls; low pressure engines. Strictly first-class in every particular. Foremost and famous for the safety, speed and regularity of schedules.

CONNECTIONS AT JACKSONVILLE WITH RAILROAD AND STEAMSHIP LINES, DIVERGING

at Tocoi, with St. Johns Railway for St. Augustine; at Palatka, with Florida Southern Railway for Gainesville, Micanopy, Ocala, Silver Springs, Leesburg, Brooksville, and stations on Charlotte Harbor Division, also with Palatka and St. Augustine Railway; at Rolleston, with St. Johns and Halifax Railway for Ormond, Daytona, and landings on Halifax river; at Astor, with the St. Johns and Eustis Division Florida Southern Railway for Kismet, Altoona, Ravenswood, Ft. Mason, Eustis, Tavares, Lane Park and landings on Lakes Harris, Eustis and Griffin; at DeLand Landing, with Railway for DeLand; at Blue Springs, with Blue Springs, Orange City and Atlantic Railway for Orange City, Lake Helen, New Smyrna, and landings on Halifax and Hillsborough rivers; at Sanford, with South Florida Railroad for stations thereon and its connections for points on the Gulf of Mexico, Key West and Havana; at Enterprise, with St. Johns, Atlantic and Indian River Railroad for Titusville, Rock Ledge, and landings on Indian river.

W. M. DAVIDSON,
General Traffic Agent
People's Line.

D. H. ELLIOTT,
Gen. Frt. & Pass. Agt.
DeBary Line.

JACKSONVILLE, FLA.

SINCLAIR'S

✻ REAL ESTATE AGENCY. ✻

ORLANDO,

ORANGE COUNTY,   FLORIDA.

100,000 ACRES OF

CHOICE LAND FOR SALE IN THE

Lake Region and Orange Belt of Florida.

Loans negotiated and investments made.   Lands surveyed and titles examined by competent persons connected with the agency.

SEND FOR DESCRIPTIVE LIST OF FLORIDA LANDS.

BRANCH OFFICE AT

TAVARES, ORANGE COUNTY FLORIDA.

THE
TROPICAL HOTEL

KISSIMMEE,

ORANGE CO., FLA.,

is situated forty miles from Sanford, on South Florida Railroad, at the head of Lake Tohopekaliga, one of the largest and most beautiful sheets of water in the State.

THE HOTEL IS HANDSOMELY FURNISHED,

the rooms being large, with open fire-places.

The cuisine will be in charge of an efficient caterer, and will be maintained, at all times, at the highest standard of excellence.

For amusements—Billiards, Boating, Lawn Tennis, etc. To the sportsman we can offer as

GOOD HUNTING OR FISHING

as is to be found in the State. Within a short distance deer and bear can be found, and English snipe, quail, and duck within one mile of town limits.

Rates per Day.	$4.00 to $3.00
Weekly Rates,	$15.00 to $21.00

SPECIAL RATES FOR THE SEASON.

PLANT STEAMSHIP COMPANY,

BETWEEN

TAMPA, KEY WEST AND HAVANA.

The new and luxurious steamships "Mascotte" and "Olivette," carrying the West India Fast Mail, perform tri-weekly service between Tampa, Key West and Havana.

These steamships possess every modern device for the comfort of Passengers.

Intelligent and gentlemanly Interpreters, speaking both the English and Spanish languages fluently, meet Passengers at Jacksonville and accompany them through to Tampa, or Havana.

Through Sleepers, New York to Tampa, via Atlantic Coast Line, only sixty-five (65) hours from New York to Havana.

Direct connections at Tampa from Havana and Key West, with South Florida Railroad, for all points North and West.

West India Fast Mail train on South Florida Railroad, south bound, makes direct connections on Steamer's sailing days, at Tampa, for Key West and Havana.

Through tickets on sale at all the principal ticket offices throughout the country.

Baggage checked through.

For further information and sailing dates, see Folders and advertisements.

H. S. HAINES,
General Manager.

C. D. OWENS,
Traffic Manager.

LAWTON BROS., Agents,
Havana, Cuba.

THOS. B. DICK, Agent,
Tampa, Fla.

www.ingramcontent.com/pod-product-compliance
Lightning Source LLC
Chambersburg PA
CBHW032032090426
42733CB00031B/729